TASTY, HEALTHY MEAT-FREE MEALS

VEGAN KIDS

100 RECIPES EVERYONE WILL LOVE

TASTY, HEALTHY MEAT-FREE MEALS

VEGAN KIDS

100 RECIPES EVERYONE WILL LOVE

HEATHER WHINNEY

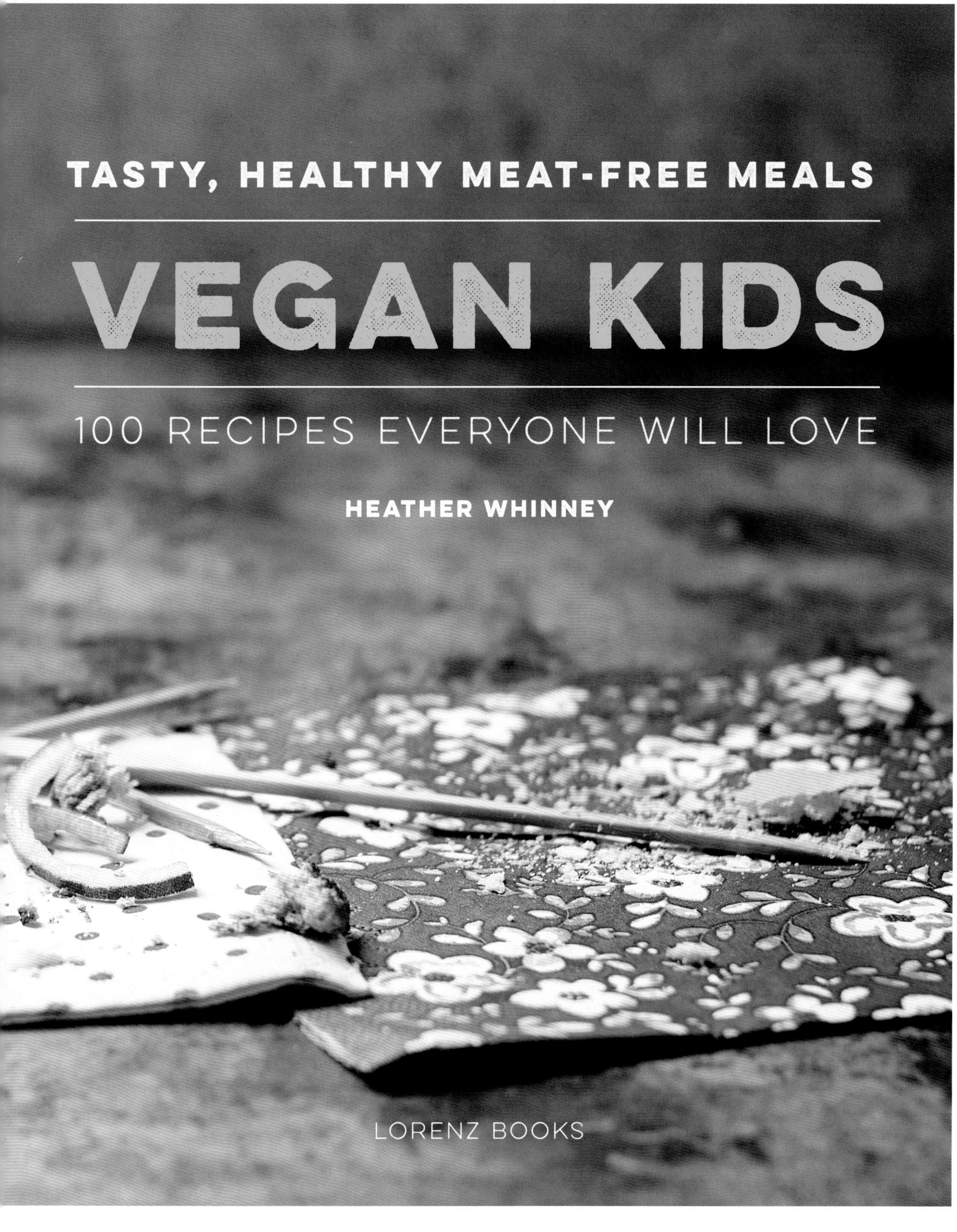

LORENZ BOOKS

CONTENTS

INTRODUCTION

As more and more children and young adults opt to become vegan, so the age-old question of 'what's for dinner' has become more difficult to answer. Just because they are vegan doesn't mean that kids will eat all (or even many) vegetables. Most still want to chomp on the burgers, pizzas and cakes they have enjoyed in the past, but now in a way that fits their ethical and dietary choices. This is where this book comes in: it is aimed not at adults who will willingly graze on kale chips or tuck into spice-laden vegetable stir-fries – fantastic though those are – but at everyday families struggling to meet the competing demands and appetites of different people, in a short amount of time, and often on a budget. With this in mind, it is packed with 101 quick, easy and tasty recipes that children will want to eat. Most of the dishes are very healthy – the fact that they are home-made means there are no hidden nasties – but the focus is also on the yum factor that will make mealtimes a pleasure. Sometimes ready-made vegan products are suggested for the sake of convenience, but there are also recipes here for making your own big vegan hitters, including sausages, burgers and 'bacon'. Making your own can be cheaper and healthier, but there is also the benefit that you can tweak the ingredients to suit your preferences. Hate herbs? Leave them out. Like things hot (or not)? Crank up or chill out the chilli.

What does it mean to be vegan? In essence, you don't consume something that causes direct or indirect harm to animals. Meat, fish, eggs, dairy and foods that contains anything derived from animals (such as gelatine) are off the menu. Many people take up vegan eating as a way of combating the damaging environmental impact of our meat-based agriculture. There are many aspects to veganism, but the focus of this book is the vegan diet: how to ensure you achieve a healthy balance of nutrients while offering up something that is going to appeal to kids and adults alike.

The introduction to the book is packed with advice on a vegan diet, and how to get the nutrients the body needs – especially for growing children and teenagers. It's important to have a broad understanding of what a 'healthy' diet is, and which foods make up the various food groups. Vitamins and minerals are also critical, and a few major ones – vitamin B12, iron and calcium – can sometimes be lacking in a vegan diet if you aren't careful to include them.

Fortunately, going vegan is a good way to focus the mind on a healthy diet. More thought is required, and conscious choices do need to be made about the food that is eaten. Since the majority of vegan food is plant-based, it is likely to be nutritious, although it's still best to avoid over-snacking on crisps and fries (which might be vegan but aren't always healthy). Some planning is needed to ensure that all the food groups are covered, but this doesn't have to be complicated. You may also choose to use supplements and multivitamins to provide a nutritional safety net, although it is considered best to get your nutrients from food sources as they are usually more readily absorbed by the body in this form. The following pages provide information about which natural foods are good sources of the various key components that our bodies need.

As well as explaining the different food groups, and why they need to be included, there's a handy guide to all sorts of plant-based products, from the huge range of dairy replacements, and how to solve the egg issue, to meat substitutes and protein-packed plant-based products such as tofu, tempeh and seitan.

So, whether you or your youngster fancy bangers and mash, or burritos, mac 'n' cheese or chocolate cake, there's something here to tempt even the fussiest eater and, most importantly, allow you all to feel good – about the food on your plate and where it came from.

A HEALTHY DIET

Broadly speaking, the current healthy eating advice is that one-third of your daily food should consist of vegetables and fruit, one-third of starchy carbohydrates, one-sixth of protein, and the remainder mostly given over to dairy alternatives and a tiny amount of oils and spreads. Another approach is to look at the nutrients that foods provide and to break them down into a few groups: protein; carbohydrates; fibre; fats; minerals; vitamins. All are essential, but not in equal proportions, and not all sources are equally good for you. We'll take a closer look at each so you can make informed choices about what you put on the table.

PROTEIN

A common misconception about veganism is that you won't eat enough protein. This isn't the case! There are so many fantastic protein-rich foods that can be enjoyed, from lentils, legumes, nuts, seeds and some grains as well as all the products derived from these, such as tofu, tempeh, and the many soya and nut milks, yogurt, creams and cheeses, even before looking at the foodstuffs that are based on them, such as veggie burgers and the rest. The big bonus with these foods is that they often contain either no fat, or else high levels of beneficial fats – unlike protein from animal sources, which tends to be high in saturated fat. What's more, they are incredibly versatile and there is a huge array within each category. Just think how many types of bean and lentil exist, and then all the different ways they can be cooked and prepared. The same applies to nuts and seeds.

CARBOHYDRATE

Carbs are an essential source of energy for our bodies: they are the fuel that keeps us going. As for all of these nutrient groups, however, there are better (unrefined or complex) and less-good (refined) types in terms of how they affect your body. It's best to go for wholewheat carbs rather than refined ones – so brown bread, pasta and rice over white types – and avoid eating too much sugar. If you do fancy something sweet, choose natural sugars that come with other benefits of nutrients and fibre, as is the case with fruit and dried fruit.

Vegetables contain varying amounts of carbohydrate, and this is where you should get much of your daily carb intake from, since veg contain so many other beneficial things, too. Fill your plate with colour! Starchy vegetables such as sweet and white potatoes, parsnips, corn, squashes and beetroot are all excellent sources of carbs, and luckily they are tasty and very versatile.

Pasta, bread, rice and other grains, such as quinoa, bulgur, couscous and barley, are also key foods in this group, and form the mainstay of many vegan dishes. The big advantage with these is that they are cheap, easy to use, and can be cooked and combined in countless ways. They are also inherently fat free, although it is usual to combine them with some oil or fat of some kind to make them more palatable. With the high carb content of these and the starchy vegetables comes a high calorie count, which is good for growing youngsters, up to a limit. It's worth checking, however, what the recommended daily intake is for different ages, depending on activity level, and try to make sure that they don't fill up on potatoes or pasta alone and instead meet nutritional requirements by eating a wide range of foods from all the groups.

FIBRE

Vegetables, fruit, grains, pulses, nuts and wholewheat foods are packed with fibre, so vegans really do have a head start when it comes to ensuring they are getting enough since these are the foods that star in most vegan dishes. Fibre is sometimes called roughage and has a whole host of

Good Foods to Eat

GOOD SOURCES OF PROTEIN

NUTS AND SEEDS pumpkin seeds, peanuts, hemp seeds, almonds, sesame seeds, pistachio nuts, sunflower seeds, chia seeds, flaxseeds/linseeds, cashew nuts, hazelnuts, walnuts

BEANS AND LEGUMES soya beans, edamame, lentils, black-eyed beans, aduki beans, butter/lima beans, kidney beans, pinto beans, haricot/navy beans, chickpeas

GRAINS seitan, amaranth, barley, quinoa, wheat berries, wholewheat pasta, oatmeal, wild rice, buckwheat, millet, couscous

VEGETABLES AND FRUIT peas, broccoli, avocados, kale, collard greens, corn, artichokes, sweet potatoes, white potatoes, Brussels sprouts, dates, guavas, pomegranates, raisins

PROTEIN PRODUCTS tempeh, tofu, spirulina, protein powders, wheat germ

GOOD SOURCES OF CARBOHYDRATE

NUTS AND SEEDS chestnuts, coconut, cashew nuts, sunflower seeds, pumpkin seeds, sunflower seeds, pistachio nuts, sesame seeds

WHOLEGRAINS amaranth, barley, buckwheat, quinoa, oats, oatmeal, brown rice, rice bran, spelt, sorghum, sprouted grains, wholewheat bread, rye bread, bran flakes, wholewheat pasta, lentil pasta, brown couscous, wholegrain crackers, rice cakes

BEANS AND LEGUMES baked beans, chickpeas/garbanzos, pinto beans, red kidney beans, cannellini beans, all lentils

STARCHY VEGETABLES sweet potatoes, white potatoes, beetroot/beet, corn, pumpkins, squashes, yams, cassavas, plantains, parsnips

FRUIT bananas, apples, mangos, dates, raisins

GOOD SOURCES OF FIBRE

NUTS AND SEEDS chia seeds, almonds, sunflower seeds, pistachio nuts, coconut, walnuts, pumpkin seeds

WHOLEGRAINS popcorn, oats, barley, oatmeal, quinoa, amaranth, buckwheat, brown rice, rice bran, spelt, sorghum, sprouted grains, wholewheat bread, rye bread, bran flakes, wholewheat pasta, brown couscous, wholegrain crackers, rice cakes

BEANS AND LEGUMES split peas, black beans, lentils, lima beans, chickpeas, kidney beans, edamame, baked beans

VEGETABLES artichokes, Brussels sprouts, kale, spinach, carrots, beet, broccoli, tomatoes

FRUIT avocados, raspberries, blackberries, apples, pears, strawberries, bananas, blueberries

GOOD SOURCES OF FATS

MONOUNSATURATED FATS are mostly found in avocados, nuts and olive, rapeseed/canola and peanut oil. **POLYUNSATURATED FATS** are mostly found in soybean and corn oil, pumpkin seeds, sesame seeds, pine nuts and dark green leafy vegetables

health benefits: it keeps you feeling full for longer, helps your digestive system work properly (i.e. keeps you regular!), and is thought to help prevent heart disease, type 2 diabetes, stroke and bowel cancer. It also feeds the good bacteria in your gut, helping your microbiome to function properly.

For maximum fibre, keep the skins on your potatoes (bake or boil them in their skins) and go for wholewheat bread, pasta, noodles and brown rice. Go for raw, unblanched nuts where possible, especially almonds, and if you want a super-healthy fibre-packed snack, get popping that corn – it's one of the fibre superstars.

FATS

There are several different types of fats, some of which are good for you and some of which should be restricted. The four main groups are saturated fats; trans fats; monounsaturated fats; and polyunsaturated fats. In very broad terms, saturated fats and trans fats (synthesized fats created through a process called hydrogenation) lead to high cholesterol levels in the body and are not good for your heart, whereas monounsaturated and polyunsaturated fats help to lower cholesterol and are good for your heart, although they should also be eaten in moderation. The first two types tend to be solid at room temperature, whereas the second two tend to be liquid, although this is only a general guide.

The good news is that a major source of saturated fat in the average diet is animal fats, so by eliminating meat and dairy you are already lowering your intake. The bad news is that some of the best fats, called omega-3 fatty acids, are found in oily fish and eggs, so you need to ensure that you obtain this from alternative sources. The other types of omega fatty acids, such as omega-6 and omega-9, are found in nuts, avocados and oils, so these aren't such an issue in a vegan diet. Besides, omega-6 is only needed in small amounts, as too much can be bad for you, and the body can synthesize omega-9 for itself, so it's called a 'non-essential' nutrient.

MINERALS

Our bodies need 16 essential minerals, and since they can't be manufactured by the body, we have to get them through our diet. We only need very tiny amounts of some kinds (trace minerals), but much higher levels of other types (major minerals), which are stored and used in the body. Minerals have various functions but predominantly regulate the body and maintain a healthy immune system. The vast majority of these are found in foods that are included in a vegan diet, but a few are harder to obtain in sufficient levels, notably iron and calcium. Since red meat is the most common source of iron, vegans – and especially children, teenagers and those who menstruate – need to look elsewhere for good sources or else they may suffer from anaemia. Note that you also need to ensure you are getting plenty of vitamin C alongside the iron since this helps the body to absorb the iron. People usually get calcium from dairy, so again, you have to make sure you are getting enough from other sources, as it is vital for children with growing bones and teeth, and very important for teens, to reduce the future risk of osteoporosis.

VITAMINS

Our body needs vitamins to work properly, and each vitamin has a different role to keep our bodies healthy. The levels required vary depending on health, lifestyle and age. Vitamins and minerals do not provide energy but assist in the release of energy provided by carbohydrates, fat and protein.

Vitamins are either water-soluble or fat-soluble. Fat-soluble vitamins A, D, E and K are stored in the liver for some time. Water-soluble vitamins B complex and C, cannot be stored by our bodies and therefore must be replaced on a daily basis. The B vitamins are needed for a healthy metabolism and nervous system, and energy production. It is recommended that vegans take a daily supplement to ensure their intake is sufficient, especially of B12. Try to get enough vitamin D from the sun and perhaps take a supplement in autumn and winter.

Minerals & Vitamins

GOOD SOURCES OF MINERALS

IRON fortified cereals, dark green vegetables, wholegrains, such as wholemeal bread and brown rice, beans, lentils, dried fruit such as apricots, figs, prunes

CALCIUM oranges, dried apricots and figs, nuts, sesame seeds, baked beans, green leafy vegetables, products fortified with calcium

ZINC nuts, tofu, wholegrains, pumpkin seeds, sesame seeds and tahini, beans and lentils

IODINE seaweed can be an excellent source but the levels of iodine vary dramatically (5g is the recommended daily amount); kelp in particular should be eaten in moderation, since this contains the highest levels. As with vitamin B12, The Vegan Society recommend a trusted regular supplement to guarantee a reliable and safe supply of iodine

GOOD SOURCES OF VITAMINS

VITAMIN A carrots, squash, sweet potatoes, yellow, orange and red bell peppers, mangoes, papayas, apricots, leafy green vegetables such as kale, spinach, watercress

VITAMINS B2, B3, B6 AND B12 cereal, wholegrains, almonds, sesame seeds, spinach, fortified vegan milks, mushrooms, beetroot, greens, quinoa, buckwheat, prunes, bananas, watermelon, peanut butter, sweet potatoes, green peas, avocados, hemp seeds, chia, beans, rice, chickpeas, wheat germ, sunflower seeds, pineapple, water chestnuts, squash, pumpkin, Brussels sprouts, green beans, pistachio nuts

VITAMIN C tomatoes, bell peppers, broccoli, kiwi, blackcurrants, kale, papaya, spring/collard greens, cranberry juice, strawberries, Brussels sprouts, broccoli, cabbage, mangetouts, cantaloupe melons, grapefruit, mangoes, oranges, watercress, raspberries, cauliflower, potatoes, pineapple, spinach

VITAMIN D fortified vegan milks, margarines, breakfast cereals, mushrooms that have been exposed to sunlight

VITAMIN E sunflower oil, rapeseed oil, peanut/groundnut oil, fortified margarines, spreads and vegan butters, hazelnuts, almonds, sunflower seeds, peanuts, peanut butter, pistachios, avocados, butternut squash, canned tomatoes, wheat germ, mangoes, broccoli, spinach, kale, chickpeas, fortified cereals

VITAMIN K leafy green vegetables such as kale, spinach, cabbage, watercress, broccoli, Brussels sprouts, lettuce, asparagus, fresh coriander/cilantro, green beans, peas, cauliflower, runner beans, leeks

A NOTE ABOUT WATER

The importance of water is often taken for granted, yet it plays a vital role in the body: it transports nutrients, regulates the body temperature, transports waste via the kidneys, and also acts as a lubricating fluid. A shortage of water can cause headaches, tiredness and loss of concentration. Most people do not drink enough: it is thought that a child aged 9–13 requires 1.2–1.75 litres/2–3 pints per day, and older children need even more.

THE VEGAN KITCHEN

Welcome to the world of vegan cooking! You've entered a wonderful, delicious and exciting way of eating. Although vegetables undeniably form the basis of many meals, they definitely aren't the only ingredients that are used to make tasty vegan food. Pasta, rice, noodles, breads, beans, pulses, grains, nuts, seeds, fruits and all sorts of plant-based dairy alternatives are all stars of the show, and that's before we get on to the huge and growing range of vegan meat alternatives that are readily available in supermarkets. So, what should you keep in stock in your cupboard?

FRUIT AND VEGETABLES

When it comes to fruit and vegetables, it's impossible to write a definitive list as it depends so much on personal taste, what the recipe requires, the season, and where you live. However, there are few hero ingredients that are appear in loads of recipes, and that it's always worth having in the kitchen.

KEEP IN STOCK onions, garlic, carrots, celery, potatoes, sweet potatoes, canned tomatoes, passata/strained bottled tomatoes, tomato paste, frozen peas, lemons, apple sauce, canned pears, dried dates, dried apricots.

NUTS AND SEEDS

Nuts and seeds are a good source of protein, healthy fat and fibre, although each nut has its own unique nutritional quality. Many are full of vitamins including E and Bs. They are great for cooking or snacking, but they can go rancid if kept too long, so don't buy too much at once. Store them in sealed jars or airtight containers in the fridge.

KEEP IN STOCK peanuts, cashew nuts, pecan nuts, almonds, macadamia nuts, hazelnuts, Brazil nuts, walnuts, chia seeds, sunflower seeds, pumpkin seeds, hemp seeds, flax seeds.

BEANS AND PULSES

These nutrient powerhouses are a good source of protein, fibre and vitamins and form the basis of many vegan meals – from burgers, dhals and casseroles to salads and much more besides. Canned beans are most convenient, as they are instant – and chickpeas/garbanzos offer the added advantage of coming in an incredibly useful liquid called aquafaba (see page 20). Dried beans and pulses need to be soaked and cooked for a few hours, so planning ahead is required, but they are cheaper, less bulky to store and sometimes provide a better texture (for hummus, for example).

KEEP IN STOCK chickpeas/garbanzos, black-eyed beans, butter/lima beans, cannellini beans, red kidney beans, baked beans, red, green and brown lentils.

PASTA AND NOODLES

You can always make a meal from these, whether it's simple pasta and tomato sauce or a noodle stir-fry. Most dried pasta is egg free, but always check the label. Note that lots of noodles do contain egg, so it's sometimes safest to go for rice noodles or mung bean noodles and again, check the pack. Choose wholemeal types for higher fibre.

KEEP IN STOCK all shapes and sizes of pasta, egg-free noodles, rice noodles, mung bean noodles.

GRAINS

These are not only cheap and versatile, but they are also packed with all sorts of nutrients and form an important part of a vegan diet.

KEEP IN STOCK brown and white basmati rice, Arborio rice (risotto), wild rice, bulgur wheat, quinoa, barley, popcorn, oats, oatmeal, amaranth, buckwheat, rice bran, spelt, sorghum, sprouted grains.

BREAD, CRACKERS & RICE CAKES

Along with rice, bread is a fundamental food that has been eaten by people all over the world for thousands of years. And with good reason: it's cheap, filling, nutritious, versatile and, if you get the right one, delicious. Go for wholewheat varieties if you can, since these are much more nutritious, and sourdough is even better if you want a happy gut. The same goes for crackers and rice cakes – choose granary, wholewheat, multi-seeded and brown types, or ones made from lentils or other pulses, since these not only taste more interesting but also contain loads of good stuff.

KEEP IN STOCK bread for slicing, wraps or flat breads, burger buns, multi-seeded crackers, rice cakes, lentil cakes.

OILS, VINEGARS & CONDIMENTS

It's amazing what a difference a trickle of olive oil or a pinch of sea salt can make to a dish, so having these flavour enhancers to hand is vital if you want to produce really delicious food. Nutritional yeast in particular is worth a mention, since it has so many benefits: it is packed with vitamins, especially B vitamins, but also lends a cheesy, umami taste to food, which is super-helpful if you want to recreate a cheesy flavour for a sauce. Stir the yeast powder into sauces, stews and soups at the end of the cooking time to retain the maximum nutrients, rather than cooking it.

KEEP IN STOCK vegetable oil (rapeseed/canola is a great multi-purpose one), extra virgin olive oil (for trickling and salad dressings), sesame oil, chilli oil, white wine and balsamic vinegars, salt (fine and sea salt), fresh black pepper, dried herbs, vegan stock/bouillon cubes, nutritional yeast, dried herbs (parsley, thyme, oregano or a ready-mixed blend), ground spices (cumin, coriander, turmeric, garam masala, cayenne, paprika, cinnamon, mixed/apple pie spice), vegan Worcestershire sauce, ketchup, soy sauce, yeast extract, vegan mayonnaise, garlic paste.

BAKING INGREDIENTS

In addition to the usual suspects – flour, sugar, fat and raising agents – vegan baking requires just a couple of specialist ingredients to provide an alternative to eggs, such as flaxseeds, vinegar and aquafaba (the liquid from canned chickpeas).

KEEP IN STOCK rolled oats, plain/all-purpose flour, self-raising flour, baking powder, bicarbonate of soda/baking soda, unsweetened cocoa powder, vegan chocolate, ground spices, caster/superfine sugar, brown sugar, icing/confectioner's sugar, golden/light corn syrup, dark treacle/molasses, agave syrup, maple syrup, sweetened condensed coconut milk, nut butters, vanilla extract, flaxseeds, apple cider vinegar, canned chickpeas, egg replacer.

FREEZER STANDBYS

Loading up the freezer with plenty of vegan foods will make mealtimes much easier. Not only is it a good idea to double up on many of the recipes in this book and freeze half to provide an instant meal on another day, but it also makes sense to load it up with these useful ingredients. Not to mention basics of oven fries, peas, corn, and dairy-free ice creams!

KEEP IN STOCK vegan sausages, vegan burgers, grated vegan cheese, breadcrumbs, aquafaba, broccoli, cauliflower, bell peppers, chopped onions, chopped herbs, chopped ginger, vegan pastry, mixed berries.

READY-MADE PRODUCTS

This is an expanding market, and you can buy vegan versions of almost anything – mince, burgers, sausages, bacon, chicken, pulled pork, sausage rolls, fish fingers, you name it! These are handy protein-packed standbys, and have the benefit of being familiar and quite similar to non-vegan versions, which can be helpful if a child is fussy, or even just when you're in a hurry. It's best to mix things up though and not rely solely on these products for your protein. Also check labels for the salt levels, which may be quite high, especially for a child.

DAIRY ALTERNATIVES

Dairy foods are one of the major food groups excluded in a vegan diet, but thankfully there are loads of excellent plant-based alternatives that you can buy, and many can be used in very similar ways to their dairy counterparts.

NON-DAIRY MILKS

For many vegans, finding a milk alternative is a top priority. The choice is mostly down to personal preferences but you may also want to consider the nutritional benefits and price of different milks, and how they work in certain things. For instance, barista oat milk is generally most successful for frothy coffees, whereas coconut milk from a carton is best in desserts and shakes.

SOYA MILK Soya beans, also known as edamame beans when eaten fresh from the pod, are the basis of soya milk (and a number of other vegan products including tofu, miso and tempeh). A good source of protein, calcium and several vitamins, soya milk is made by soaking, blending, cooking and filtering the beans, and is one of the most common types of non-dairy milks. NB: soya milk can be a problem for those with a thyroid condition as it can interfere with the absorption of medication, so always leave at least 4 hours after taking thyroid tablets before consuming soya milk or soya milk products.

NUT MILKS There are lots of different types of nut milk – almond, hazelnut, walnut, macadamia, pecan, pistachio and Brazil nut – although the most popular and widely consumed is almond milk. This has a silky-smooth texture and creamy taste as well as fantastic nutritional benefits. Its mild flavour makes it perfect for drinking, pouring over cereals and for cooking. Hazelnut, pistachio and macadamia have a rich texture and nutty flavour, making them a luxurious choice for creamy desserts and milkshakes. Try to go for an unsweetened type.

PEA MILK Thick and rich, milk made from yellow split peas is high in protein (around eight times as much as store-bought almond milk) as well as being a good source of calcium and iron. It has a creamy-white colour and mild, neutral flavour – nothing like peas – and is made in a very different way to nut-based milks. In commercial pea milk, the yellow peas are milled into flour and processed, separating the pea protein from the starch and fibre. The protein part is then blended with water and a little oil and often fortified with vitamin B12. It's particularly good from an environmental perspective as peas requires far less water for growing than do nuts such as almonds.

OAT MILK Oat milk can be a good option for those with allergies or intolerances as it is free of lactose, nuts, soya and gluten (if made from certified gluten-free oats). It also contains beta-glucan, a soluble fibre that can help reduce cholesterol. It is simple and inexpensive to make, but commercial varieties have the advantage of often being fortified with calcium and vitamins. If you buy it, choose unsweetened if possible.

RICE MILK This can be made from white or brown rice and has a neutral flavour. It contains less protein than nut and seed milk, but it is good blended with nut milks or used in dishes where a more delicately flavoured non-dairy milk would be wasted or a more strongly flavoured one would be overpowering.

COCONUT MILK This is usually bought in cans and is a blend of thick and thin coconut milk. Every brand is slightly different, and the fat content can vary between ½–1 tbsp per 100ml/3½fl oz. Many contain additives such as thickeners, stabilizers and emulsifiers. Coconut milk can also be bought in powdered form, which can be reconstituted to the desired thickness with water. This is particularly

useful if you only require a small amount of coconut milk. It is typically mixed with double the amount of water to powder, but can be made with less water if you want to enrich a dish with coconut milk without diluting it. You can also buy coconut milk in a carton, which is intended for drinking or using as you would dairy milk.

EVAPORATED COCONUT MILK & CONDENSED COCONUT MILK These can be directly swapped for their dairy counterparts. They have a mild coconut taste, but this is hardly noticeable when they are combined with other ingredients.

Barista!

Your choice of plant-based milk to use in hot chocolate, coffee and tea is a personal one. Many find that a light soya milk or cashew milk works well and those who take sugar may enjoy coconut or almond milk as these have a slightly sweet flavour. You can also buy 'barista blends', which are designed to be frothed to create latte and cappuccino-style coffees. Always allow hot drinks to cool for 2–3 minutes before adding plant-based milks to reduce the likelihood of curdling.

MARGARINE AND BUTTERS

Plant-based vegan margarine and butter can be substituted for dairy versions weight for weight in recipes. A range of non-dairy spreads is available, most of which are suitable for spreading, baking and shallow-frying, unless stated otherwise on the packaging.

SOFT MARGARINE Sold as spread, this is great for, well, spreading, and in cakes that involve you creaming together butter and sugar. It is also fine for use in cooking – for frying and for making sauces – but can be less successful for making pastry or anything for which you have to rub together fat and flour.

HARD VEGAN MARGARINE OR BUTTER Margarine is also sold in hard blocks like butter, and this is best if you need to rub together any ingredients. A vegan hard butter is good if the butter is going to be a star flavour – for instance for melting on corn cobs or in a jacket potato, and in buttercream.

COCONUT COOKING BUTTER Made from puréed coconut flesh, this white solid product is sold in jars and can be used in place of dairy butter in most recipes. It is not the same as coconut oil, which is extracted from the coconut, although oil can also be used in cooking and baking.

NUT AND SEED BUTTERS There are many different types, crunchy and smooth, and they have multiple uses – in sauces, for baking, or simply spread on toast for a protein hit. Jars of peanut and (if more expensive) almond butter are a great storecupboard standby. A delicious nut cream can be made by blending nut butter with water or another liquid.

NON-DAIRY CHEESE

Finding cheese substitutes is becoming easier by the day as brands expand their ranges and new products come on to the market. That said, if you were once a dairy-cheese lover and connoisseur, you will have to accept that non-dairy cheese isn't quite the same. It is difficult to make plant-based ingredients taste and melt like dairy cheese rather than the vegetable oils, nuts, tofu, coconut and nutritional yeast they are made from; it is better to accept and enjoy vegan cheeses for their own merits and find out by trial and error which types and brands suit your personal preferences, whether you are want a vegan cheese to eat with crackers or to use in cooking.

MILD CHEESES In the chilled aisle of supermarkets, you will typically find blocks of cheese, packets of wrapped slices ready for sandwiches or grilling or broiling, and bags of ready-grated cheese. The base for these is usually a soya blend, coconut oil or brown rice protein, and they are intended to be the equivalent of dairy cheeses such as Cheddar and mozzarella, with mild, neutral flavours. They also come in flavoured forms, such as tomato and basil, mixed herb or smoked.

GREEK-STYLE CHEESE If you love your feta and fancy a Greek salad, this is the plant-based product for you. It's made with coconut oil and can be diced into cubes.

VEGAN CREAM CHEESE This handy product, usually made with coconut oil, is readily available and very versatile. It also now comes in many different flavours, from cracked black pepper to chocolate!

SPECIALIST CHEESES Vegan cheeses from smaller specialist makers tend to be sold online or in vegan stores. They are mostly made from nuts, and often come in 'fresh' and 'fermented' types. These vary from melting mozzarella-types to harder grating ones, although you can also buy cheeses akin to squidgy Brie as well as fermented blue-veined cheeses, and even ones flavoured by the addition of liquid smoke or truffle oil. They can be more expensive than standard supermarket types however and are generally intended for the cheeseboard rather than everyday cooking.

NON-DAIRY YOGURT

Vegan yogurts are typically made with soya, nut or coconut milks, with or without the addition of probiotics. They are also sometimes thickened with cornflour/cornstarch, and sweetened with sugar or syrup, or flavoured. They can usually be used interchangeably with different dairy yogurts. Make sure you buy an unsweetened type for using in savoury dishes.

FERMENTED YOGURT Most vegan yogurts are fermented, since this gives them the desired sourness and tang. Happily, it also makes them easier to digest, and this, together with the probiotics that are sometimes added (look for 'live' types) means they are great for our guts.

COCONUT YOGURT Made primarily from coconut cream, this yogurt is especially thick and creamy, and most like dairy Greek-style strained plain yogurt. It's delicious on its own, but also tends to be less likely to split when added to curries and sauces than other types of vegan yogurt.

NON-DAIRY CREAM

When it comes to cream, it's possible to buy vegan equivalents for most types of dairy.

SOYA CREAM This is the most versatile of the creams, and comes in single/light, double/thick, whipping and aerosol form.

SOUR CREAM Often made from soya cream or blended silken tofu, it is also very easy to make your own from double soya cream by adding a squeeze of lemon (or even a spoon of apple cider vinegar).

OAT CREAM Naturally thick and creamy, oat creams are available as single/light cream and crème fraîche.

PLANT DOUBLE CREAM This product is made with fava beans and vegetable oils, and is very useful since it can be poured and whipped, in the same way as double/heavy dairy cream.

COCONUT CREAM This is the thick creamy part of coconut milk that rises to the top of the can, in the same way that cream comes to the top of cow's milk. You can either buy coconut cream, or put a can of coconut milk in the fridge for a few hours and then skim off the thick cream at the top. (Choose full-fat coconut milk not the reduced-fat variety.)

EGG SUBSTITUTES

Traditionally used in batters, quiches, custards, sauces, ice creams, desserts and cakes, eggs help to thicken, aerate, bind or emulsify ingredients and as such are fairly important in non-vegan cooking. This may sound alarming, given that eggs are not part of the vegan diet, but fortunately, there are alternatives that work just as well. The key is that different recipes require different approaches and not all substitutes are interchangeable.

FLAX & CHIA SEEDS

High in protein and omega-3 fatty acids, the outer layer of flax and chia seeds is a mucilage; a sticky layer found in most plants to aid water storage. When combined with water, a gel emulsion is created, which binds ingredients together. To make the equivalent of 1 egg, mix 1 tbsp ground flaxseed (or linseed) with 3 tbsp cold water and leave to soak for at least 5 minutes. The seeds will absorb the liquid, creating a thick, gloopy texture. You can buy ready-ground flax, or grind your own to a fine powder using a pestle and mortar, coffee grinder or spice grinder.

Chia seeds can be used in the same way (again mixing 1 tbsp seeds with 3 tbsp water). There's no need to grind them first, but you can if you prefer a finer texture and don't want tiny seeds in the finished dish. White chia seeds can be used rather than black ones for light-coloured bakes. Only use flax and chia seeds as an egg replacer in recipes that need no more than 2 eggs.
GOOD FOR pancakes, brownies, muffins and cookies.

NUT BUTTER

Smooth peanut, cashew, almond and sunflower butters can be used as a replacement in recipes where eggs are purely used to hold the mixture together. They add both protein and a nutty flavour. Replace 1 egg with 3 tbsp nut butter but be aware that the nut butter won't 'set' mixtures in the same way as eggs, so the resulting bakes will have a softer texture.
GOOD FOR cookies, cakes and traybakes.

AQUAFABA

Translating as 'water bean', this is a lovely name for the unpromising-looking liquid in a can of chickpeas. It can be used as an emulsifier or binder but is best known for its ability to be whisked to create a thick foamy mixture similar to whisked egg whites. Using juice from the can is the easiest method, though slowly cooking dried beans in a minimal volume of water for several hours will give the same results. Use 3 tbsp aquafaba for 1 egg, 2 tbsp for 1 egg white, or 1 tbsp to replace 1 egg yolk.
GOOD FOR as an emulsifier in vegan mayonnaise, and whisked to make pipeable meringues, macarons, Yorkshire puddings, and airy mousses or ice creams.

CHICKPEA FLOUR

Also known as garbanzo bean flour, besan, chana or gram flour, pale brown chickpea flour is high in protein and can be used to both bind and help aerate baked goods. To replace 1 egg, blend 3 tbsp chickpea flour with 3 tbsp plant-based milk.
GOOD FOR baked custard-type mixtures, cakes, muffins and scones.

TOFU

Soft-set tofu called 'silken' tofu is a good substitute for milk or cream and egg mixtures. Use 65g/2½oz silken tofu for 1 egg, blending until smooth and creamy before use.
GOOD FOR cheesecakes, creamy tarts, brownies, and cakes with a heavier and moist texture.

BICARB & VINEGAR

Bicarbonate of soda/baking soda reacts with vinegar to produce lots of foamy bubbles that, when combined with vegan milk, produces surprisingly light eggless cakes and bakes. Use 1 tsp bicarbonate of soda mixed with 1 tsp vinegar to replace 1 egg and add an extra 3 tbsp plant milk to the mixture.
GOOD FOR cakes and plain baked goods.

FRUIT & VEGETABLE PURÉES

Puréeing or mashing fruit and vegetables is a flavourful way to replace eggs as it not only helps bind the mixture together but also provides moisture and sweetness. For the equivalent of 1 egg, use 1 mashed banana or 65g/2½oz puréed avocado or cooked and puréed apple, sweet potato, butternut squash or pumpkin.
GOOD FOR reduced-sugar and reduced-fat bakes.

AGAR AGAR

Extracted from red algae, this is often used instead of gelatine to set jellies and vegan cheeses. A recipe may have to be adapted if it would usually be baked. Agar agar has no colour, taste or aroma and is activated by being boiled in liquid for 5 minutes.
GOOD FOR custard-based fillings for tarts, crème caramel and panna cotta.

VEGAN EGG REPLACER

This is a commercial fine white powder made from a blend of potato starch, tapioca starch, a raising/leavening agent and cellulose. A 450g/1lb pack is the equivalent of about a hundred eggs. Reconstituted with water, it mimics the properties of whole eggs, yolks and egg whites in cooking and baking. It may not always work with your own recipes and it is better to follow those created for the product. As 'egg whites', the mixture will be softer, and not suitable for defined piping.
GOOD FOR cakes, bakes, quiches, batters and meringues.

Vegan Mayonnaise

As with all mayonnaise, you can buy jars of ready-made, but it's also easy to make your own delicious version when needed for dipping and dolloping. It will keep for up to a week in the refrigerator.

MAKES 250 ML/8 FL OZ

PREP 10 MINS

45ml/3 tbsp aquafaba (the liquid from a can of chickpeas)

1–2 tsp Dijon mustard

½ tsp salt

a pinch of ground white pepper

15ml/1 tbsp apple cider vinegar or white wine vinegar

1 tsp lemon juice

200ml/7fl oz/scant 1 cup light olive or sunflower oil

1 Put the aquafaba, mustard, salt, pepper, vinegar and lemon juice in a food processor or blender and blend for a few seconds until combined.
2 With the motor running, very slowly drizzle in the oil, making sure that it is fully combined before adding more. If the top starts to look slightly oily, stop adding oil for a few seconds and continue blending.
3 Continue to drizzle in the oil; the aioli will suddenly thicken. Once all the oil is added and thoroughly blended, add the lemon juice and garlic.
4 Spoon the mayonnaise into a glass or stainless-steel (not plastic) container, bowl or sterilized jar, cover well (so the flavour doesn't transfer to other foods), and chill until ready to serve.

MEAT ALTERNATIVES

If you feel the need for something 'meaty', there are now lots of ready-made plant-based options to choose from, from sausages and burgers to gougons. New brands and products are being developed all the time, so try them out and see which you prefer. They make excellent quick vegan meals, and are included in some of the recipes, but can be quite expensive and processed. There are also soya-bean products that are a good source of protein.

TOFU

This is made from soaked, mashed and strained soya beans. It is white, milky and set in custard-like squares. Its texture can be soft (silken tofu) or firm. Fresh tofu should be kept covered with water in the refrigerator; change the water daily and use within a week. Vacuum-packed, long-life tofu can be stored unopened at room temperature. Freezing is not recommended as this alters the texture. One of the joys of cooking with plain tofu is that it absorbs the flavours of other ingredients well during cooking. Smoked and marinated tofu are also available.

FIRM TOFU This lightly pressed product is sold in water or vacuum-packed, and can be cubed or sliced. Use it in stir-fries, stews and soups, crumbled into salads, or even barbecued. It is also excellent as a substitute for scrambled eggs.

SILKEN TOFU This is the softest, most delicate form of tofu. A creamy version comes in tubs and can be used for dips, dressings or sweet dishes, such as fruit fools and non-dairy ice cream. A slightly firmer type of silken tofu comes in cubes, which break down very easily, so handle carefully.

FRIED TOFU At first glance, this doesn't look much like tofu, but slice the nut-brown block and the white interior is exposed. The outer colour is the result of deep-frying in vegetable oil, a process that adds flavour, and makes the beancurd more robust.

TEMPEH

This is made by fermenting cooked whole soya beans in banana leaves, which gives the product a nutty, savoury flavour and causes it to solidify so that it can be cut into blocks. The beans remain visible under a velvety coating. It is available chilled or frozen. Like firm tofu, tempeh benefits from marinating and can be used in many of the same ways – in stir-fries and kebabs, for example. Its firmer texture also makes it an excellent meat substitute in casseroles, pies and baked dishes.

TEXTURED VEGETABLE PROTEIN (TVP)

This is manufactured from soya beans into different shapes and forms. It has a firm, sponge-like texture and can be flavoured to resemble meat or, alternatively, can be left as a natural soya product. TVP needs to be rehydrated with water or stock before being incorporated into recipes. It is fortified with vitamin B12.

VITAL WHEAT & SEITAN

Vital wheat is the protein-rich part of wheat that is left when the starch is washed away from normal wheat flour. It can be used to add bulk and protein to vegan foods, but is most easily used in the form of seitan, which is dough made from vital wheat and water, that is boiled to create a chewy ball with a convincing 'meaty' texture. It doesn't taste of much, but absorbs flavour well, and is used to manufacture lots of ready-made meat alternatives.

JACKFRUIT

Used for its texture, which is slightly stringy, like pulled pork or chicken, jackfruit is useful for bulking up dishes, although it does not contain any protein. Buy young green fruit in brine, not syrup.

EASY MEALS

Some meal planning can help you explore and experiment with new dishes as well as ensure that you are getting all the nutrients you need.

BREAKFASTS

Always start the day with a balanced breakfast, including at least one piece of fruit. Stick to one or two regular cereals if that is easy and healthy – home-made muesli, granola or porridge with a sprinkling of seeds and berries is perfect. Do check labels on cereal packets as many seemingly healthy products contain large amounts of sugar.

* Wholewheat toast is good but include some protein-rich nut butter, or a sprinkle of seeds to keep you going longer.
* Porridge is the ultimate breakfast, especially in the winter, since it keeps you full for ages and is good for you. Mix in some dried fruit and nuts, or top with fresh berries or some stewed fruit.
* Add diced fresh fruit, berries, dried fruit, nuts and seeds to live vegan plain yogurt.
* Try scrambled tofu on a bagel with some vegan 'bacon' on the side.

LUNCHES & LIGHT MEALS

It's important to take time to stop for lunch to refuel for the rest of the day. Avoid having to resort to fast food or being stuck because there aren't any vegan options, by packing your lunch the night before.

* Vegan soup in a vacuum flask with a bread roll and a small container of grated vegan cheese makes a fantastic lunch in cold weather.
* Another simple lunch is small pasta shapes in a tomato sauce, or mixed with vegan pesto. Include a small container of grated vegan cheese or chopped-up vegan sausage to stir in, or if you are home, you can heat them together.
* Sandwiches are an easy choice. There are lots of filling ideas on pages 108–111. If you're at home try a hot toastie or quesadilla (pages 105–6).
* Include some crudités and perhaps some protein-rich hummus (see page 173).
* Raisins, berries, grapes, satsuma segments and chopped apple are easy and appetizing.
* A sweet treat is always welcome, and it's better to eat something home-made. There are lots of ideas in the baking chapter, but remember you can't take anything containing nuts into school.

MAIN MEALS

Base your main meal around a high-protein complex carbohydrate, such as wholemeal pasta, quinoa, barley, basmati rice, noodles, or starchy veg such as sweet potatoes. Choose your vegetables and add a protein element to your meal, perhaps tofu, seitan, chopped nuts or seeds, or ready-made falafel, vegan bacon or sausages. And make the recipes in this book! You'll never get bored and there's something for everyone, whether you have a passion for pizza or prefer oodles of noodles.

SNACKS

Although there is a big range of ready-made vegan-friendly snacks, it's usually cheaper and healthier to make your own, to your personal tastes.

* Dried fruit, seeds and nuts are an easy snack, though don't take nuts to school.
* Popcorn, packed with fibre and vitamins, is a great snack option (see page 183).
* Energy balls are the bomb! Try the ones on 228 and 231, and have them ready in the freezer.
* Make your own crisps! Jazz things up by making them from beet or parsnip (see page 181).
* Smoothies are fantastic for getting some of your five fruit and veg a day (see page 155).

PASTA
NOODLES
PIZZA
&
RICE

SPAGHETTI VEGANESE

Spag bol is a real crowd-pleaser that's easy to prepare in advance and make in big batches – perfect for busy family life. This colourful vegan version uses lentils, which provide feel-full meatiness and flavour as well as being packed with protein and fibre, and tasty mushrooms for extra oomph.

SERVES 4 * PREP 15 MINS * COOK 50 MINS

1. Heat the oil in a large, heavy pan, then add the onion, season with salt and pepper and cook on a low heat for about 10 minutes or until softened. Stir in the garlic and cook for a further minute.
2. Stir in the celery, carrot and oregano and cook for 5 minutes, adding a drizzle more oil if it starts to dry out. Next, add the mushrooms and cook for 4 minutes, stirring occasionally.
3. Add the lentils, tomato paste, chopped tomatoes and stock, give it a stir, then bring it to the boil. Reduce to a simmer and cook for 20–30 minutes, until most of the stock has been absorbed. Top up with a little hot water if it seems too dry.
4. While that is cooking, bring a large pan of salted water to a steady boil, add the spaghetti for 10–12 minutes or according to the packet instructions, until just tender. Drain well.
5. To serve, divide the spaghetti up between serving plates, spoon over the lentil mixture and top with grated cheese, if you like.

COOK'S NOTES

* This tastes even better the next day! Leave it to cool, then store it in a sealed container in the fridge until you're ready to use it. Reheat it thoroughly in the microwave on high for about 6 minutes, stirring it halfway through the time.

* To get ahead, make double the quantity and freeze half in a suitable container. Leave it to thaw, then reheat it in a pan – the mushrooms will release moisture when they thaw and you may need to cook off the excess water.

1 tbsp vegetable oil

1 onion, peeled and finely chopped

2 garlic cloves, peeled and finely chopped

2 celery sticks, finely chopped

2 carrots, peeled and finely chopped

a pinch of dried oregano

200g/7oz chestnut mushrooms, finely chopped

400g/14oz can of brown or green lentils, drained and rinsed

1 tbsp tomato paste

400g/14oz can of chopped tomatoes

500ml/17fl oz/2 cups hot vegetable stock

salt and ground black pepper

400g/14oz dried spaghetti

115g/4oz/1⅓ cups vegan hard cheese, grated (optional)

Look Out!

Most dried pasta is egg-free, but it is always worth checking the label to be sure.

PASTA WITH SWEET TOMATO SAUCE & CRISPY 'BACON'

You can't beat a simple pasta and tomato sauce dish – everyone in the family always loves it! This is made sweeter with the addition of a few sun-dried tomatoes and grated carrots, while the crispy vegan 'bacon' provides texture and protein.

SERVES 4 * **PREP 10 MINS** * **COOK 40 MIN**

1. Preheat the oven to 200°C/400°F/Gas 6. Lay out the vegan 'bacon' slices on a baking sheet, drizzle with a little of the oil and put in the oven to cook for 15–20 minutes or as per packet instructions. When cooked, remove and chop into pieces.

2. Meanwhile, pour the remaining oil into a large, heavy pan, add the onion and cook for about 8 minutes, until beginning to soften, then stir in the garlic and cook for a further 2 minutes. Add the carrot and sun-dried tomatoes and stir so everything gets coated. Cook for a couple more minutes.

3. Tip in the tomatoes and vinegar and squash the tomatoes with the back of a spoon. Bring to the boil, then reduce to a simmer and cook gently for 30–40 minutes. The sauce will reduce and the flavour will intensify. Taste and adjust the seasoning as needed.

4. While the sauce is simmering, put the pasta in a large pan of boiling salted water and cook for 10–12 minutes, or according to the packet instructions, until just tender. Turn off the heat, drain well and return the pasta to the pan.

5. When you're ready to serve, add the sauce to the pasta and toss well together, then transfer to bowls for serving. Top with 'bacon' pieces, and garnish with basil if you like.

COOK'S NOTES

* This will make plenty of sauce, so you could freeze some. Leave it to cool, then put it in a sealed container, label and freeze for up to 3 months. Defrost overnight in the fridge before using.

* Sprinkle over vegan parmesan cheese or nutritional yeast flakes for an extra flavour boost.

- 4–6 vegan 'bacon' slices
- 1 tbsp vegetable oil
- 1 onion, peeled and finely chopped
- 2 garlic cloves, peeled and finely chopped
- 2 carrots, peeled and finely grated
- 4 sun-dried tomatoes, finely chopped
- 2 × 400g/14oz cans of plum tomatoes
- a splash of red wine vinegar
- salt and ground black pepper
- 400g/14oz tagliatelle or dried pasta of your choice, to serve
- a few basil leaves, to garnish (optional)

SPAGHETTI 'CARBONARA'

Classic carbonara sauce is made with egg yolks, cream and Parmesan cheese. This vegan version combines silken tofu and vegan milk to make a deliciously rich sauce without the dairy. The final flourish is a scattering of carrot 'bacon', which has a lovely smoky flavour and crispy texture.

SERVES 4 * PREP 20 MINS + 20 MINS MARINATING * COOK 30 MINS

350g/12oz spaghetti

FOR THE CARROT 'BACON'

2 large carrots, peeled and trimmed
1 tbsp tahini
1 tbsp vegetable oil
2 tsp maple syrup
1 tsp dark soy sauce
1 tsp liquid smoke

FOR THE CARBONARA SAUCE

250g/9oz silken tofu
120ml/4fl oz/½ cup vegan milk
5 tbsp nutritional yeast flakes
1 tbsp lemon juice
1 tbsp tahini
1 tsp white miso paste
½ tsp ground turmeric
salt and ground black pepper

1. To make the carrot 'bacon', slice the carrots lengthways using a vegetable peeler to get thin, even slices. Mix the tahini, oil, maple syrup, soy sauce and liquid smoke together in a bowl. Add the carrot slices and mix with your hands to coat all over. Cover the bowl and marinate the carrot strips at room temperature for about 15 minutes.

2. Preheat the oven to 180°C/350°F/Gas 4. Line a baking sheet with baking parchment. Arrange the carrot slices on the baking parchment and bake for 10–12 minutes or until dark golden and crisp, turning over halfway through the cooking time. Leave to cool.

3. For the pasta, bring a large pan of salted water to the boil, add the spaghetti and cook for 10–12 minutes or according to the packet instructions, until just tender.

4. Meanwhile, for the carbonara sauce, blend the tofu, milk, nutritional yeast, lemon juice, tahini, miso and turmeric together in a blender until very smooth. Season to taste.

5. Drain the spaghetti in a colander, reserving 4 tbsp of the cooking liquid. Cover the colander with the pan lid to keep it hot. Return the reserved cooking liquid to the pan and heat until steaming. Pour in the carbonara sauce and bring to the boil, stirring. Turn off the heat, and gently stir in the pasta.

6. Divide the spaghetti between warmed bowls, adding a few pieces of carrot 'bacon' to each. Serve immediately with a grinding of black pepper.

COOK'S NOTE

Liquid smoke is distilled from burning wood, and a few drops adds a hickory seasoning. Most are vegan but check the labels.

COURGETTI WITH CLASSIC PESTO

This classic vegan green pesto is made with a blend of pine nuts, olive oil, fresh basil and garlic – a wonderful mix of fragrant flavours. This recipe makes more than you will need, so you'll have some left over to keep in the fridge for another meal. The spiralized veg are delicious and of course count towards your daily vitamin intake, but are also pretty and a bit different from pasta.

SERVES 4 * PREP 15 MINS * COOK 10–12 MINS

1. To make the pesto, roughly tear the basil leaves and place them in a food processor with the garlic, pine nuts and 2 tbsp of the oil. Whiz until the mixture is fairly smooth. Alternatively, place the ingredients in a mortar and pestle, and pound into a paste. Reserve 2 tbsp of the oil and gradually work the rest into the basil mixture.

2. Transfer to a bowl and stir in the grated cheese and the lemon juice. Season to taste.

3. Spiralize the courgettes and carrot using the 3mm/⅛in (medium) spiralizer noodle blade. If you do not have a spiralizer, cut the courgettes and carrot into fine strips.

4. Bring a large pan of salted water to the boil. Add the potato cubes, bring back to the boil and simmer, covered, for 7 minutes. Add the carrot noodles and when the water comes back to the boil, add the courgette noodles. Cook for a further 3 minutes or until all the noodles are tender.

5. Tip into a colander and drain thoroughly, shaking gently for a minute to allow some of the steam to evaporate. Tip the vegetables back into the pan and heat gently for a few seconds to evaporate any juices that leak from the courgettes.

6. Spoon over about half of the pesto sauce, stir to coat all the vegetables, then serve straight away on warm plates. Garnish with basil sprigs, if you like.

7. Store the unused pesto in a clean glass jar, topped with the 2 tbsp reserved olive oil. It will keep in the fridge for up to 2 weeks.

3 large courgettes/zucchini, preferably a mixture of green and yellow, about 800g/1¾lb

1 large carrot, peeled and trimmed

1 medium waxy potato, peeled and cut into 1cm/¾in cubes

sprigs of fresh basil, to garnish

FOR THE PESTO SAUCE

leaves from a large bunch of basil, about 40g/1½oz

2 garlic cloves, peeled

50g/2oz/½ cup pine nuts

120ml/4fl oz/½ cup extra virgin olive oil

25g/1oz/⅓ cup vegan hard cheese, grated, plus extra to serve if you like

2 tsp fresh lemon juice

salt and ground black pepper

GREEN PESTO PAGE 40
RED PESTO PAGE 44
ORANGE PESTO PAGE 43

PESTO PASTA 3 WAYS

Pesto pasta is perfect for a quick mid-week meal. Making your own pesto means you can be sure it is vegan, and it allows you to experiment with different flavours. It's also a great way to boost your veg and nut intake. The classic pesto is made with fresh basil, pine nuts, olive oil, garlic and 'cheese', as shown in the recipe on page 37, but there are so many variations to try. Come up with your own combinations!

* Basil is traditional in pesto but all kinds of fresh leafy herbs work well and add their distinctive individual tastes – coriander/cilantro, parsley and little salad greens like rocket/arugula, baby spinach, and even nasturtium leaves!
* Grated vegan cheese adds the savoury seasoning, but you can provide umami hits with ingredients like nutritional yeast flakes, garlic powder, sea salt and freshly ground peppercorns.
* Experiment with different seeds and nuts, which add nutrition as well as flavour and texture; you could try toasted pumpkin seeds, sunflower seeds and sesame seeds.
* Getting the right taste and consistency to your pesto means adding the oil slowly and tasting it as you go – then you can adjust the flavour to suit, adding more salt and pepper, or more or less oil.

Storing!

Fresh pesto will keep in the fridge for 3–4 days; keep in a glass jar and top with a little olive oil.

INSTANT MEALS

Pesto is so versatile: as well as saucing all kinds of pasta shapes, it can be stirred into a tomato sauce to add flavour, slathered on to a pizza or flatbread as a base for other toppings, layered in a veggie bake, or mixed into rice – add some green peas and sweetcorn and you have a 'risotto'. You can add a dollop of pesto to a baked potato, spread a layer in a sliced tomato sandwich or into a tortilla wrap, with hummus and salad. Or just melt a spoonful into a bowl of hot minestrone, vegetable or tomato soup.

PASTA WITH GREEN PESTO

This vivid green pesto offers a change in flavour to the more traditional sauce (on page 37), as it includes lots of broccoli as well as the fresh basil, and toasted cashew nuts are used instead of pine nuts; walnuts also work well!

SERVES 4 * PREP 15 MINS * COOK 15 MINS

400g/14oz dried pasta

FOR THE GREEN PESTO

250g/9oz broccoli florets

125g/4¼oz/1 cup cashew nuts

leaves from a large bunch of basil, about 40g/1½oz

2 garlic cloves, peeled

50g/2oz/⅔ cup vegan hard cheese, grated, plus extra to serve if you like

2 tbsp nutritional yeast

about 4 tbsp extra virgin olive oil

salt and ground black pepper

1. Put the broccoli in a pan of boiling salted water and cook for 5 minutes or until just tender. Drain really well and leave to cool.

2. Meanwhile, toast the nuts. Put them in a heavy frying pan and heat until they are beginning to turn golden. Alternatively, spread them out on a baking sheet and cook at 200°C/400°F/Gas 6 for 5 minutes, until golden.

3. Put the broccoli, most of the basil (save a few leaves for a garnish), salt and pepper, garlic, cheese, nutritional yeast and cashew nuts in a food processer and whiz until combined. Drizzle in the oil and whiz until you get the right consistency. Alternatively, place the ingredients in a mortar and pestle, and pound into a paste. Taste and season some more if it needs it, and add a splash more oil if the mixture is too thick.

4. For the pasta, bring a large pan of salted water to the boil, add the pasta and cook for 10–12 minutes or according to the packet instructions, until just tender.

5. Drain the pasta well, return it to the pan and toss with the pesto. Transfer to serving bowls, with a sprinkling of extra grated cheese if you like.

VARIATION

To make creamy green pesto, blitz a few spoonful of soya cream cheese with it before tossing it with the pasta.

PASTA WITH ORANGE PESTO

This lovely orange pesto is full of flavour and has a wonderful sweetness to it thanks to the roasted butternut squash, which makes it appealing for fussy eaters. Packed with vitamins and fibre, it's also really good for you. What's not to love?

SERVES 4 * **PREP 20 MINS** * **COOK 30 MINS**

400g/14oz dried pasta

FOR THE ORANGE PESTO

½ butternut squash, seeded, peeled and cubed

5 tbsp extra virgin olive oil

150g/5oz/1 cup pine nuts

a pinch of chilli flakes (optional)

2 garlic cloves, peeled

50g/2oz/⅔ cup vegan hard cheese, grated, plus extra to serve if you like

2 tbsp nutritional yeast flakes

a few basil leaves

salt and ground black pepper

1. Preheat the oven to 200°C/400°F/Gas 6. Put the butternut squash in a roasting pan, toss with 1 tbsp of the olive oil and season with salt and pepper. Add a pinch of chilli flakes, if you like a little heat. Put the pan in the oven and roast for about 20 minutes, until golden and tender, then remove from the oven and put to one side.

2. While the squash is roasting, toast the pine nuts by spreading them out on a baking sheet and roasting them in the oven for about 5 minutes, or until golden. Remove and set aside to cool. You can also toast them in a heavy frying pan, being careful not to let them burn.

3. Put the toasted pine nuts, garlic, cheese, nutritional yeast, basil leaves, salt and pepper in a food processor and whiz until combined. Drizzle in the remaining 4 tbsp of olive oil and whiz, then add in the butternut squash and use the pulse button a few times so it retains some texture and is a little chunky. Alternatively, place the ingredients in a mortar and pestle, and pound into a coarse paste. Taste and season again if needed.

4. For the pasta, bring a large pan of salted water to the boil, add the pasta and cook for 10–12 minutes or according to the packet instructions, until just tender.

5. Drain the pasta well and toss with the pesto. Transfer to bowls and serve, sprinkled with extra cheese if you like.

COOK'S NOTE

The trick when making this pesto is to only use the pulse button on the food processor so you can control it. You want to keep some texture rather than turning it into a smooth purée.

PASTA WITH RED PESTO

Sweet roasted red bell peppers whizzed to a textured purée with walnuts make a delicious pesto for pasta, or tossed with some roasted vegetables. The balsamic vinegar really helps to balance the sweetness of the peppers and the slight bitterness of the nuts.

SERVES 4 * PREP 20 MINS * COOK 45 MINS

1. Preheat the oven to 200°C/400°F/Gas 6. Put the peppers in a roasting pan and toss with 1 tbsp of the olive oil. Put in the oven and cook for about 30 minutes or until the peppers begin to blister and blacken slightly.

2. While the peppers are roasting, toast the walnuts by spreading them out on a baking sheet and toasting them in the oven for about 5 minutes, or until golden. Remove and set aside to cool.

3. Remove the peppers from the oven and carefully slide them into a plastic bag – the peppers will steam and the skins will come away easily. When cool enough to handle, skin the peppers and put the flesh in a food processor. (Or to speed things up, you can use ready-roasted peppers from a jar.)

4. Add the walnuts, garlic, cheese, nutritional yeast, balsamic vinegar, salt and pepper, and whiz to combine. Trickle in the remaining 4 tbsp of olive oil and whiz until the sauce is the right consistency. Alternatively, place the ingredients in a mortar and pestle, and pound into a paste. Taste and season some more if it needs it.

5. For the pasta, bring a large pan of salted water to the boil, add the pasta and cook for 10–12 minutes or according to the packet instructions, until just tender.

6. Drain the pasta well and toss with the pesto. Transfer to bowls and serve, sprinkled with cheese and an extra grinding of black pepper, if you like.

VARIATION: SUN-DRIED TOMATO PESTO

For another easy and delicious red pesto, just substitute 225g/8oz sun-dried tomatoes for the roasted peppers, and pine nuts for the walnuts.

400g/14oz dried pasta

FOR THE RED PESTO

2 red bell peppers
5 tbsp extra virgin olive oil
115g/4oz/1 cup walnuts
2 garlic cloves, peeled
50g/2oz/⅔ cup vegan hard cheese, grated, plus extra to serve if you like
2 tbsp nutritional yeast flakes
a splash of balsamic vinegar
salt and ground black pepper

MACARONI CHEESE

This tasty pasta dish topped with a crisp layer of herby breadcrumbs should be in every vegan's repertoire. Quick and easy to make from store-cupboard ingredients, it makes a satisfying lunch or supper dish when served with a simple side salad.

SERVES 4 * PREP 15 MINS + 15 MINS INFUSING TIME * COOK 30–35 MINS

1 litre/1¾ pints/4 cups vegan milk

1 small onion, peeled and quartered

1 bay leaf

350g/12oz dried macaroni

75g/3oz/6 tbsp vegan margarine

75g/3oz/⅔ cup plain/all-purpose flour

½ tsp English mustard powder

2 tbsp nutritional yeast flakes

¼ tsp ground turmeric

50g/2oz/⅔ cup vegan Cheddar-style cheese, grated

½ bunch of fresh thyme

40g/1½oz/¼ cup fresh breadcrumbs

1 tbsp olive oil

salt and ground black pepper

1. Pour the milk into a heavy pan. Add the onion and bay leaf and heat until steaming. Turn off the heat, cover with a lid and leave to infuse for 15 minutes. Strain the milk into a jug or pitcher, discarding the onion and bay leaf.
2. Preheat the oven to 180°C/350°F/Gas 4. Cook the macaroni in a pan of salted boiling water for 10–12 minutes or according to the packet instructions, until just tender.
3. Meanwhile, melt the margarine in the pan, then add the flour, stirring continuously. Cook over a low heat for a few seconds, then turn off the heat and gradually add the warm milk, whisking continuously. Bring to a boil and simmer for 3–4 minutes, until thick and smooth. Remove the pan from the heat and stir in the mustard, nutritional yeast, ground turmeric and grated cheese.
4. Drain the macaroni, then add to the sauce, mixing well. Tip the mixture into an ovenproof baking dish measuring about 30 x 20cm/12 x 8in.
5. Pick the thyme leaves off the stalks and put the leaves in a food processor with the breadcrumbs. Season with pepper. Drizzle over the oil, then blitz for a few seconds. Sprinkle the crumb topping over the macaroni mixture.
6. Bake in the oven for 15–20 minutes or until the topping is lightly browned and the macaroni bubbling. Serve warm.

VARIATION

Ground turmeric adds just a hint of flavour to the dish, but its main purpose here is to give the sauce a pale golden cheesy colour. You can leave it out, if you prefer.

VEGETABLE LASAGNE

A hearty vegan dish packed with flavour, this is ideal for a family meal or get-together as it can be made several hours in advance. Lightly browned vegetables are layered with sheets of lasagne and tomato sauce and covered with a creamy sauce before baking.

SERVES 6 * **PREP 30 MINS + 15 MINS SOAKING TIME** * **COOK 1–1¼ HRS**

1. To make the tomato sauce, put the mushrooms in a bowl. Pour over the hot water and soak for 15 minutes. Tip the porcini and liquid into a sieve or strainer set over a bowl and squeeze the mushrooms with your hands to release as much liquid as possible. Pour the liquid through a fine sieve or strainer and reserve.

2. Heat the oil in a large frying pan, add the onion, carrot and celery and fry for about 10 minutes, until softened. Place in a food processor with the tomatoes, tomato paste, basil, porcini and soaking liquid, and blend to a purée.

3. For the vegetable mixture, heat 2 tbsp of the oil in a large frying pan and cook the courgette slices over a medium heat for 5–8 minutes, until lightly coloured all over (cook in batches if it's easier). Season to taste and put the cooked courgettes in a bowl.

4. Heat the remaining 1 tbsp of oil in the pan and cook the onion for 3 minutes. Add the mushrooms and garlic and cook for 5 minutes. Add to the courgettes. Preheat the oven to 190°C/375°F/Gas 5.

5. For the white sauce, melt the margarine in a pan, then mix in the flour and cook, stirring, for 1 minute. Gradually whisk in the milk, then bring to the boil and cook, stirring, until smooth and thick. Season to taste.

6. Spread half the tomato sauce in a shallow ovenproof dish. Next, spread over half the vegetable mixture, then one-third of white sauce, then half the lasagne sheets. Repeat these layers, topping with the remaining white sauce. Bake for 30–45 minutes, until golden and the lasagne is tender.

8 lasagne sheets

FOR THE TOMATO SAUCE

15g/½oz dried porcini mushrooms
120ml/4fl oz/½ cup hot water
2 tbsp vegetable oil
1 onion, peeled and chopped
1 carrot, peeled and chopped
1 celery stick, chopped
2 × 400g/14oz cans of chopped tomatoes
1 tbsp tomato paste
1 tsp dried basil

FOR THE VEGETABLE MIXTURE

3 tbsp vegetable oil
450g/1lb courgettes/zucchini, thinly sliced
1 onion, peeled and finely chopped
450g/1lb chestnut mushrooms, thinly sliced
2 garlic cloves, peeled and crushed
salt and ground black pepper

FOR THE WHITE SAUCE

40g/1½oz/3 tbsp vegan margarine
40g/1½oz/⅓ cup plain/all-purpose flour
900ml/1½ pints/3¾ cups vegan milk
salt and ground black pepper

STICKY TOFU NOODLES

Soft vacuum-packed udon noodles require no pre-cooking – just add them to the wok at the end of cooking. You can throw in any extra favourite veg, just make sure you cut it all into similar-sized pieces so it cooks evenly. Chopsticks at the ready, there's slurping to be had!

SERVES 4 * PREP 20 MINS * COOK 15–20 MINS

1. Mix together the sauce ingredients, toss the tofu with some of it (about 1 tbsp) and put the rest to one side.

2. Heat half the oil in a wok and add the coated tofu, stir-fry for 5–6 minutes until it starts to turn golden, then remove and put to one side.

3. Heat the remaining oil in the wok, then add the spring onion, garlic, ginger, chilli if using, and season with the salt and pepper. Cook, stirring it around the pan, for about 2 minutes.

4. Add the carrots, broccoli and beans and stir around the pan for 5–6 minutes, until the vegetables begin to become tender. Push all the vegetables to one side and add the sauce, turn the heat up a little and let it bubble, then stir everything together.

5. Now add the tofu, tomatoes and noodles and toss everything together so it all gets coated with the sauce. Cook for a further 2–3 minutes, until the noodles are heated through and the tomatoes start to soften. Season it some more if it needs it, and sprinkle with sesame seeds, if using.

COOK'S NOTES

* The trick with making stir-fries is to have all your vegetables cut and prepared so you can add them all easily to the wok as you go.

* Use the stalk from the broccoli as well as the florets – it's the best bit! Trim off the end and the harder exterior, then chop the pale inside of stalk.

FOR THE SAUCE

3 tbsp dark soy sauce

1 tbsp maple syrup

1 tbsp rice wine vinegar

1 tbsp peanut butter, smooth or crunchy

juice of 1 lime

FOR THE STIR-FRY

2 tbsp vegetable oil

375g/13oz firm tofu, pressed to remove the water and cut into chunky cubes

a bunch of spring onions/scallions, trimmed and finely chopped

2 garlic cloves, peeled and grated

5cm/2in piece of fresh root ginger, peeled and grated

½ fresh red chilli, seeded and finely chopped (optional)

2 carrots, peeled into strips

1 head of broccoli, cut into florets, stalks trimmed and chopped

150g/5oz fine green beans, trimmed and roughly chopped

6 cherry tomatoes, halved

250g/9oz ready-to-wok medium udon noodles

salt and ground black pepper

3 tsp sesame seeds, toasted, for topping (optional)

VEG NOODLE LAKSA

A laksa is a light curried soup made with a base of spices and creamy coconut milk that's packed with vegetables as well as soft noodles. It is fragrant and aromatic rather than hot and fiery, so even if you don't normally like curry you should give it a try.

SERVES 4–6 * PREP 20 MINS * COOK 30 MINS

1. First make the sauce paste. Put the onion, garlic, ginger, turmeric, coriander, cumin, garam masala, salt and pepper in a food processor and whiz to a paste. Add a little of the coconut milk and whiz again.

2. Pour the mixture into a large pan or wok, then pour in the remaining coconut milk and the stock. Bring to the boil, then reduce to a simmer, taste and season some more if needed.

3. Add the sweet potato, courgettes, carrots and green beans to the pan and cook gently for about 20 minutes or until the vegetables are tender.

4. Add the tomatoes, spinach and noodles and cook for a further 5–10 minutes, until everything is combined and piping hot. The tomatoes should squash down and the spinach will wilt.

5. Ladle into bowls, and serve topped with beansprouts and fresh coriander, along with halved slices of cucumber if liked, and wedges of lime to squeeze over.

VARIATIONS

* You could add some tofu to this if you wish. Heat 1 tbsp vegetable oil in a large frying pan, add 200g/7oz chopped tofu and fry gently until golden, turning occasionally and topping up with more oil as needed. Drain on kitchen paper, then sit the pieces on top of the soup.

* You could use mangetouts/snowpeas or sugar snap peas in place of the green beans, if preferred.

FOR THE LAKSA SAUCE

1 onion, peeled and roughly chopped
2 garlic cloves, peeled
5cm/2in piece of fresh root ginger, peeled
2 tsp ground turmeric
1 tsp ground coriander
1 tsp ground cumin
1 tsp garam masala
2 × 400ml/14fl oz cans of coconut milk
200ml/7fl oz/1 cup hot vegetable stock
salt and ground black pepper, to taste

FOR THE VEGETABLES

2 sweet potatoes, peeled and cubed
2 courgettes/zucchini, chopped
2 carrots, peeled and sliced
250g/9oz green beans
10 cherry tomatoes
225g/8oz spinach leaves
300g/11oz ready-cooked rice noodles
a handful of beansprouts
a handful of fresh coriander/cilantro leaves
½ cucumber, deseeded and sliced (optional)
lime wedges, to serve, if liked

EASY MARGARITA PIZZA

A pizza dough only requires three ingredients! The only other thing you need is a little time for the dough to rise. It's definitely worth it, as the pizzas taste so much better than bought ones. Margarita is the classic, and simplest, pizza topping – see overleaf for others.

MAKES 4 * PREP 20 MINS + 2½ HRS PROVING * 10–15 MINS PER PIZZA

1. For the dough, put the flour, salt and yeast in the bowl of a food processor fitted with a dough hook. Slowly add the warm water and mix until it is all combined. Drizzle in the oil and continue mixing on low to medium speed for about 5 minutes, until the dough starts to slap against the sides of the bowl and is smooth and elastic. If kneading by hand, combine the ingredients in a large bowl, then tip the dough on to a lightly floured surface and knead it for 10 minutes, until it is really smooth and elastic and doesn't stick to the surface.

2. Transfer the dough to a bowl, lightly greased with oil, then cover with a damp dish towel and put the bowl somewhere warm. Leave the dough for a couple of hours, until it doubles in size.

3. Remove the dough from the bowl and place it on a lightly floured surface, then press it with your knuckles until it shrinks back to its original size. Divide it into 4 equal balls. Sit these balls on a baking sheet, well spaced apart, then cover with the dish towel and leave for a further 30 minutes. Your dough is now ready to roll out, top and bake. Preheat the oven to its highest setting.

4. Roll each ball out, one at a time, using a rolling pin on a lightly floured board. You will have to stretch it with your hands too, as it will keep pinging back. Roll each ball to a large round, about 25cm/10in, then loop over the rolling pin and transfer to a large baking sheet per pizza. If you don't have 4 baking sheets, you'll have to work in batches.

5. To make the tomato sauce, simply put the tomatoes in a food processor and blitz briefly with the oil. Season.

6. Lightly spread the rounds with sauce, leaving a 2.5cm/1in edge. Scatter with the cheese and add the tomato slices. Bake the pizza(s) for 10–15 minutes or until the base is crisp and the topping cooked. Remove, garnish with basil, slice and serve.

FOR THE DOUGH

500g/1¼lb/4½ cups strong white bread flour, plus extra for dusting

1 tsp salt

7g/¼oz easy-blend/rapid-rise dried yeast

300ml/½ pint/1¼ cups warm water

3 tbsp olive oil, plus extra for greasing

FOR THE TOMATO SAUCE

400g/14oz can of whole plum tomatoes

a splash of extra virgin olive oil

salt and ground black pepper

FOR THE TOPPING

a handful of vegan mozzarella-style cheese, sliced or broken into pieces

4 tomatoes, sliced

a few basil leaves

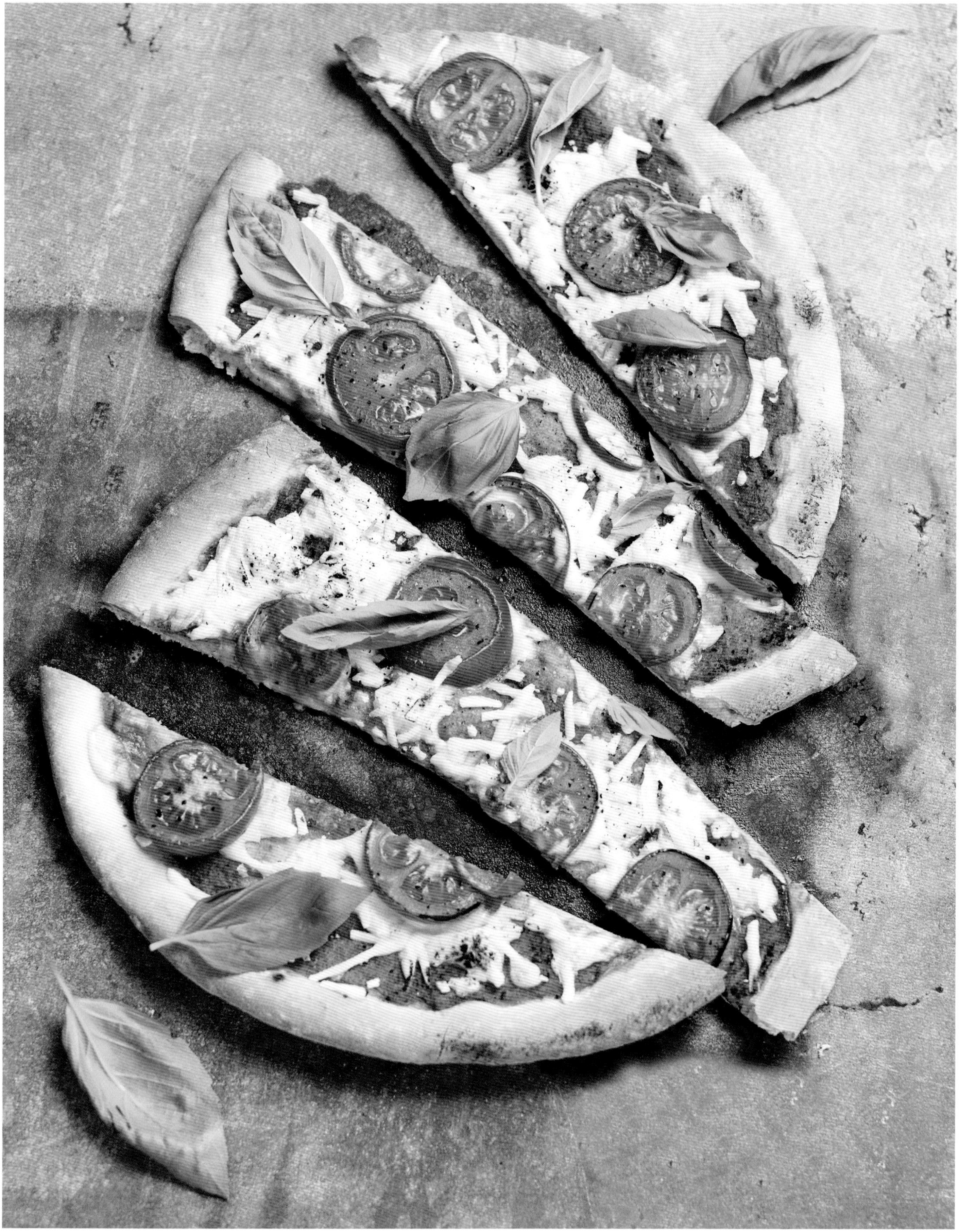

MUSHROOM &
RED PEPPER
EASY MARGARITA
PAGE 54
HAWAIIAN

PIZZA PARTY

Once you've got your pizza dough base, all you need to do is spread it with some tomato sauce, and add a selection of your favourite toppings. Keep it simple with Easy Margarita (on page 54) or get creative with mushrooms and peppers, or 'ham' and pineapple – each of the topping combinations below is enough for 1 pizza.

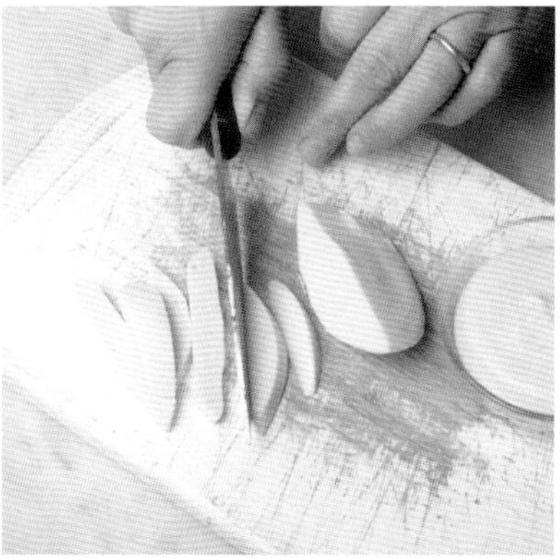

HAWAIIAN

3–4 slices of vegan 'salami' or strips of vegan 'ham'

a handful of pineapple chunks

a handful of vegan mozzarella-style cheese, sliced or broken into pieces

MUSHROOM & RED PEPPER

a handful of mushrooms, sliced

1 red bell pepper, halved, seeded and sliced into strips

a handful of vegan mozzarella-style cheese, sliced or broken into pieces

MORE TOPPING IDEAS...

* Slices of courgette/zucchini, black olives, and vegan pesto.
* Chopped vegan sausage and strips of roasted butternut squash.
* Slices of red onion, roasted aubergine/eggplant, tomato, and strips of fresh chilli.
* Add finely chopped fresh red chilli or a pinch of smoked paprika to the tomato sauce.
* If you don't want a tomato-based pizza, just leave it off and make a 'pizza bianca' (white pizza) by topping your dough with a drizzle of extra virgin olive oil, grated vegan cheese, and sliced vegetables.

PIZZA TIPS

* One thing a pizza likes is a hot oven, so heat the oven to its highest setting in plenty of time before you are ready to bake. Some bakers use a special pizza stone, as that gets really hot.
* Have all your topping ingredients sliced and ready.
* Using semolina instead of flour for dusting and rolling can help create a crisp crust.
* It's tempting to add lots of toppings but 2–3 work best.
* The tomato sauce recipe freezes really well, so why not make twice as much so you're ready to roll another time. It can also be served with pasta.

CALZONE WITH SPINACH, TOMATOES & VEGAN MOZZARELLA

A calzone is simply a stuffed and folded pizza – it's a parcel of deliciousness! Make sure you seal the edges really well or it may explode and ooze filling everywhere when it puffs up and bakes. Simply scale the ingredients up or down to make the number required.

SERVES 4 * **PREP 20 MINS (EXCLUDING THE DOUGH)** * **COOK 10–15 MINS**

1. Preheat the oven to its highest setting. Divide the dough into four and form each into a ball.

2. On a lightly floured board, roll out one dough ball into a rough circle, about 25cm/10in across. Spread with about 2 tbsp of tomato sauce, leaving a 2.5cm/1in border, then heap some spinach, tomato slices and cheese on to one half.

3. Wet around the edges of the dough with a little water, then fold it over to cover the ingredients and press the edges together really firmly. It should look like a giant pasty.

4. Dust lightly with flour then lift the calzone on to a baking sheet or sheets. Repeat for the other calzone.

5. Bake for 10–15 minutes, until crisp and golden. Be careful when you cut into the calzone, as very hot steam will come out.

plain/all-purpose flour, for dusting

1 quantity of dough (see page 54)

8 tbsp tomato sauce (see page 54)

a large handful of spinach leaves

4–6 tomatoes, sliced

a handful of vegan mozzarella-style cheese, sliced , grated or broken into pieces

FUN FRIED RICE

Get your five a day in one dish! The cauliflower rice tossed with wholegrain rice is super-tasty, so even if you think you don't like cauli, you will be a convert – it adds a sweet, nutty flavour.

SERVES 4 * PREP 15 MINS * COOK 10–15 MINS

200g/7oz vegan 'chicken' tenders, gougons or similar

2 tbsp vegetable oil

2 tbsp soy sauce

a bunch of spring onions/scallions, trimmed and finely chopped

3 carrots, peeled and diced

1 red bell pepper, halved, seeded and chopped

1 yellow bell pepper, halved, seeded and chopped

150g/5oz/1¼ cups frozen peas, defrosted

340g/11½oz can of sweetcorn, drained

1 tbsp rice vinegar

250g/9oz/1¼ cups ready-cooked wholegrain rice

200g/7oz/1 cup ready-cooked cauliflower rice

salt and ground black pepper

1. Cook the vegan 'chicken' tenders. Preheat the oven to 200°C/400°F/Gas 6 or as per packet instructions. Toss the tenders with 1 tbsp of the oil and 1 tbsp of the soy sauce, then put in a small roasting pan and cook for 6–8 minutes. Put to one side and keep warm.

2. Meanwhile, heat the remaining 1 tbsp oil in a wok or large pan, add the spring onions and toss them around. Season with salt and pepper, then add the carrots and peppers and cook for 4–5 minutes, until beginning to soften.

3. Stir in the peas and sweetcorn, the remaining 1 tbsp of soy sauce and the rice vinegar, then tip in the ready-cooked rice and cauliflower rice and stir to tumble it all together. Heat it through gently for a few minutes, tasting and adjusting the seasoning as required.

4. Transfer to serving bowls and top with the 'chicken' tenders.

Veggie Hack

It's easy to make your own cauliflower 'rice'. Chop a whole head of cauliflower into florets, put it in the food processor and whiz until fine. Transfer to a bowl, cover with clear film or plastic wrap and microwave for 3 minutes, then remove and put it to one side to cool. (Be very careful as the bowl and film will be hot and full of steam.)

SUSHI

Who says you can't have sushi if you are a vegan? These colourful rolls are fun to make and once you get the hang of the technique, you can become more adventurous with your fillings.

SERVES 4–6 * PREP 40 MINS * COOK 20 MINS

250g/9oz/1¼ cups sushi rice, rinsed

1 tbsp rice vinegar

3 tbsp vegan mayonnaise

1 tsp dark soy sauce

4–6 sheets of sushi nori seaweed

a small bowl of soy sauce, for dipping

a small bowl of pickled ginger, to serve

FOR THE FILLINGS

1 red bell pepper, halved, seeded and cut into strips

1 avocado, halved, stoned/pitted and sliced into strips

2 carrots, peeled, cut into strips and lightly cooked

1 cucumber, cut into strips

½ bunch of spring onions/scallions, cut lengthways into strips

sesame seeds

1. Put the rice in a pan with 300ml/½ pint/1¼ cups water and cook for about 20 minutes or as per packet instructions. The rice should absorb all the water. Transfer the rice to a large bowl, stir in the rice vinegar and put it to one side to cool.
2. Combine the vegan mayonnaise and soy sauce in a small bowl and put to one side.
3. When you're ready to assemble the sushi, lay out the sheets of nori seaweed, shiny side down, spread with the mayonnaise mixture, then spread the rice evenly over the top, leaving a 2cm/¾in strip of nori uncovered at the top and bottom.
4. Arrange your chosen filling ingredients in a line down one side of the rice, trying to make it all as neat and uniform as possible so you get a bit of everything in each roll when you cut it. Do the same for the another filling on another sheet of nori. One tasty combination is red pepper and avocado strips. Another is carrot, cucumber and spring onion strips. Avocado and cucumber are good, too. Sprinkle with sesame seeds if you like.
5. With wet hands, start to roll the sushi sheets up as tightly as you can. They don't have to be perfect. Cut the rolls into slices and sit them on a serving plate.
6. Serve the sushi pieces with soy sauce for dipping, and pickled ginger for those who like it.

SUMMERY RISOTTO WITH PEAS

A risotto is comforting to eat and soothing to make. It's also really adaptable – swap the vegetables with the seasons, and experiment using ingredients you know you like. This would be nice with a pinch of chilli flakes if you are a spice fan!

SERVES 4 * PREP 10 MINS * COOK 40 MINS

1 tbsp vegetable oil

2 tbsp vegan margarine

1 onion, peeled and finely chopped

2 garlic cloves, peeled and finely chopped

about 1 litre/1¾ pints/4 cups vegetable stock

250g/9oz/1¼ cups Arborio rice

a large handful of frozen peas, defrosted

75g/3oz/1 cup vegan hard cheese, grated

2 tsp nutritional yeast flakes

salt and ground black pepper

1. Heat the oil and half the margarine in a large, deep pan. Add the onion and season with salt and pepper, then cook for 10 minutes to soften. Stir in the garlic and cook for another minute.
2. Meanwhile, put the vegetable stock in a pan and bring it to a simmer. Keep it at a low simmer throughout the cooking process.
3. Add the rice to the softened onion and garlic and stir well for 1 minute so it all gets coated in the oil. Ladle in a little of the hot stock and stir in until it has been absorbed. Keep adding the stock a little at a time, stirring constantly, until it all gets absorbed and the risotto is creamy yet the rice retains a little bite.
4. When the rice is ready, stir through the peas and cook for a couple of minutes to heat through, then stir through the cheese and nutritional yeast. Taste and check the seasoning and add a little more if needed.

COOK'S NOTE

A risotto should be served just 'al dente', which means it still has a slight 'bite' to it. It should neither be too dry nor too runny. Add the stock a little at a time so that you can judge how much more it needs as the rice absorbs it.

More Risotto Ideas

Spring – asparagus and sweetcorn

Summer – tomato and olive

Autumn – pumpkin and parsnip

Winter – mushroom and leek

BURGERS GRILLS FRIES & WRAPS

TOFU & SWEET POTATO BURGER PAGE 73
BEETROOT BURGER PAGE 70
SOYA BURGER PAGE 74

BURGER BONANZA

Few things are as pleasurable as biting into a juicy burger, stuffed with all sorts of tasty fillings that you can mix and match to suit. The joy of vegan burgers is that they can be made in lots of different ways. What's more, they are much healthier than meat ones, low in fat and packed with protein, fibre and all manner of vitamins – a far cry from junk food.

* Making your own burger mix is really simple, especially if you have a food processor. The trickiest part is getting them to bind and stay together while you cook them. To fix this problem, some of these burgers use aquafaba, the liquid from a can of chickpeas, which has binding qualities and can be used as a substitute for egg in patties (and other recipes).

* Feel free to stack your burgers with your favourite veggies and vegan-friendly sauces.

* If you are topping your burger with a slice of vegan cheese, sit it on top of the patty and place under a hot grill or broiler to melt for a minute before sandwiching into the bun.

* Burgers are perfect for freezing. Layer uncooked patties between pieces of waxed paper, put them into a freezer bag or double-wrap them in plastic wrap, then stash them in the freezer for up to 1 month. Defrost them overnight in the fridge and cook as per the recipe.

Look Out!

Make sure you don't buy brioche-style burger buns since they are not vegan- friendly.

TOPPING & FILLING IDEAS

lettuce, torn

tomato, sliced

red onion, peeled and finely sliced

slaw (see page 70)

gherkins, sliced

vegan mayonnaise

mustard of your choice

vegan cheese, sliced

tomato ketchup

hummus

guacamole

BEETROOT BURGER

You make a seriously delicious burger out of beetroot. Apart from being loaded with vitamin C, it has a juicy texture and great taste. It goes brilliantly with lettuce, tomato and the crunchy cabbage slaw given here, or add your own preferred fillings and toppings to build the burger of your dreams.

MAKES 8 * PREP 30 MINS + 20 MINS CHILLING * COOK 40 MINS

1. Heat 1 tbsp of the oil in a frying pan, add the onion, season with salt and pepper and cook on a low heat for about 10 minutes or until softened. Leave to cool.

2. Put the grated beet and carrot in a couple of pieces of strong kitchen paper and, wearing gloves, squeeze over a sink to remove as much liquid as possible. Don't use a dish towel as the beetroot juice will ruin it!

3. Put the beet and carrot in a food processor, along with the chickpeas, tahini, oats and thyme, then add the cooled onions. Pulse until it all comes together, then add a little of the flour if needed and some salt and pepper, and pulse again. Drizzle in some of the juice from the chickpeas. You shouldn't need it all – just enough for the mixture to start binding together. If you don't have a food processor, put everything on your largest board and chop it all together with a large knife, scraping and blending it as you go.

4. Scoop the mixture out of the food processor, place it on a lightly floured board and divide it up into 8 portions. Wet your hands to stop the mixture sticking, and roll the portions into balls, then flatten into patties. Put on a baking sheet and place in the fridge to chill for 20 minutes.

5. Meanwhile, mix together all of the ingredients for the slaw, season to taste and put it to one side.

6. Heat a little of the oil in a large frying pan and cook 2–3 patties at a time for about 4 minutes until the underside is starting to turn golden. Flip over and cook the other side for about the same amount of time. Remove the patties, put them to one side and keep warm. Repeat until all the patties are cooked.

7. Serve the patties sandwiched in a lightly toasted burger bun with the slaw and any other toppings you like.

3–4 tbsp vegetable oil

1 onion, peeled and finely chopped

4 cooked beetroots, grated

1 carrot, peeled and grated

400g/14oz can of chickpeas/garbanzos, drained but keep the liquid

1 tbsp tahini

75g/3oz/scant 1 cup rolled oats

a few thyme stalks, leaves only

1 tbsp plain/all-purpose flour, plus extra for dusting

salt and ground black pepper

8 burger buns, halved and lightly toasted, to serve

lettuce and tomato slices, to serve

FOR THE SLAW

½ small white cabbage, finely shredded

½ red cabbage, finely shredded

300g/11oz/1½ cups vegan plain yogurt mixed with 1 tsp Dijon mustard

salt and ground black pepper

TOFU & SWEET POTATO BURGER

These tofu, bean and roasted sweet potato burgers are super-satisfying and packed with protein and fibre. Their sweet flavour means they appeal to even the fussiest eaters, and they are easy to make, too. You can make them even tastier by layering them with lots of salad fillings and a dollop of hummus.

MAKES 8 * PREP 30 MINS + 20 MINS CHILLING * COOK 50 MINS

1. Preheat the oven to 200°C/400°F/Gas 6. Toss the sweet potato in 2 tsp of the oil, season with salt and pepper, and roast in the oven for about 20 minutes until golden and tender. Remove and put to one side to cool.
2. Heat 1 tsp more of the oil in a frying pan, add the onion and cook on a low heat for about 10 minutes or until softened, then put to one side to cool.
3. Put the cooled roasted sweet potato, tofu, beans, oats, breadcrumbs, soy sauce, paprika and cooled onions in a food processor and season with salt and pepper. Pulse until thick and combined, then add the flour a little at a time and pulse again, adding a little more flour if necessary, until if forms a smooth paste. If you don't have a food processor, put everything on your largest board and chop it all together with a large knife, scraping and blending it as you go.
4. Scoop the mixture out of the food processor (if using), place it on a lightly floured board and divide it up into 8 portions. Wet your hands to stop the mixture sticking, and roll the portions into balls, then flatten them into patties. Put the patties on a baking sheet and place in the fridge to chill for 20 minutes before cooking.
5. When you are ready to cook the patties, heat a little of the oil in a large frying pan and cook 2–3 patties at a time for about 4 minutes or until the underside is starting to turn golden. Flip them over using a spatula and cook the other side for about the same amount of time.
6. Remove the patties, put them to one side and keep warm. Continue until all the patties are cooked.
7. Serve sandwiched in a lightly toasted burger bun with toppings of your choice.

400g/14oz sweet potato, peeled and roughly chopped

3–4 tbsp vegetable oil

1 onion, peeled and finely chopped

200g/7oz firm tofu, pressed to remove the water

400g/14oz can of black beans, drained

3 tbsp rolled oats

3 tbsp fresh breadcrumbs

a splash of soy sauce

2 tsp paprika

1 tbsp plain/all-purpose flour, plus extra for dusting

salt and ground black pepper

8 burger buns, halved and lightly toasted, to serve

hummus, lettuce, red onion slices and tomato slices, to serve

SOYA BURGER

Packed with protein, these classic soya burgers have such a 'meaty' texture and umami flavour that it's hard to believe they are vegan. As ever, add toppings of your choice – perhaps slices of red onion, salad, and a slice of melting vegan cheese.

MAKES 8 * PREP 30 MINS + SOAKING + 20 MINS CHILLING * COOK 40 MINS

- 225g/8oz/1 cup soya mince
- 3–4 tbsp vegetable oil
- 1 onion, peeled and finely chopped
- 400g/14oz can of kidney beans, drained
- 4 tbsp chickpea/gram flour
- 115g/4oz/2 cups fresh breadcrumbs
- 3 tsp smoked paprika
- a pinch of chilli flakes (optional)
- 1 tbsp yeast extract
- 3 tbsp liquid from a can of chickpeas/garbanzos
- 1 tbsp plain/all-purpose flour, plus extra for dusting
- salt and ground black pepper
- 8 burger buns, halved and lightly toasted, to serve
- vegan Cheddar-style cheese slices, hummus, lettuce, tomato and red onion slices, to serve

1. Rehydrate the soya mince with hot water according to the packet instructions, then drain well. Or if using frozen mince, defrost the amount required.

2. Heat 1 tbsp of the oil in a frying pan, add the onion, season with salt and pepper and cook on a low heat for about 10 minutes or until softened. Put to one side to cool.

3. Put the kidney beans, chickpea flour, breadcrumbs, paprika, chilli flakes (if using) and yeast extract in a food processor. Pulse until thick and combined, then add the soya mince and pulse to combine. Drizzle in enough chickpea liquid (aquafaba) so that the mixture comes together. Add a little flour if needed. If you don't have a food processor, put everything on your largest board and chop it all together with a large knife, scraping and blending it as you go.

4. Scoop the mixture out of the food processor (if using), place it on a lightly floured board and divide it up into 8 portions. Wet your hands to stop the mixture sticking, and roll the portions into balls, then flatten them into patties. Put the patties on a baking sheet and place in the fridge to chill for 20 minutes before cooking.

5. When you are ready to cook the patties, heat a little of the oil in a large frying pan and cook 2–3 patties at a time for about 4 minutes or until the underside is starting to turn golden. Flip them over using a spatula and cook the other side for about the same amount of time.

6. Remove the patties, put them to one side and keep warm. Continue until all the patties are cooked, adding a little more oil as you go.

7. Serve sandwiched in a lightly toasted burger bun with toppings of your choice.

FISHLESS FINGERS AND CHIPS

There's no need to miss out on the fun on fish Friday! Coating tofu in crunchy breadcrumbs whizzed up with dried seaweed gives it a fabulous 'fishy' flavour. Serve it up with a pile of peas and fries of your choice, and get stuck in.

SERVES 4 * PREP 30 MINS * COOK 20–30 MINS

1. Preheat the oven to 200°C/400°F/Gas 6. Pat the tofu with kitchen paper to dry it well, then slice it into fingers.
2. Put the nori and breadcrumbs in a food processor and whiz until well combined and fine. If you don't have a food processor, put everything on your largest board and chop it all together with a knife.
4. Prepare the chips (see overleaf), and while they are cooking, prepare the 'fish'.
5. Pour the milk into a shallow dish, and tip the seaweed breadcrumbs on to a plate. Dip the tofu strips in the milk to coat, then toss in the breadcrumbs. Place them on a lightly greased baking sheet and put them in the oven to cook for 20 minutes or until golden. (If you are also making chips, put the tofu strips into the oven about half way through the chips' cooking time so they are ready together.)
6. Meanwhile, put the peas in a pan of lightly salted water and cook for about 5 minutes, until tender, then drain and bash slightly with a pinch of salt.
7. Serve up the 'fish', chips and peas with some ketchup on the side, if you like.

375g/13oz firm tofu, pressed to remove the water

2 sheets of nori seaweed

115g/4oz/2 cups fine fresh breadcrumbs

4–5 potatoes for your choice of chips (see page 79)

about 2 tbsp vegan milk

a little vegetable oil

225g/8oz/2 cups frozen peas

salt

ketchup, to serve (optional)

SWEET POTATO CHIPS
SKINNY FRIES
FAT CHIPS

EASY FRIES 3 WAYS

Everyone loves fries, and cooking them in the oven avoids deep-frying and hot oil. Make them fat and thick, thin and crisp, or out of sweet potatoes for a flavoursome change.

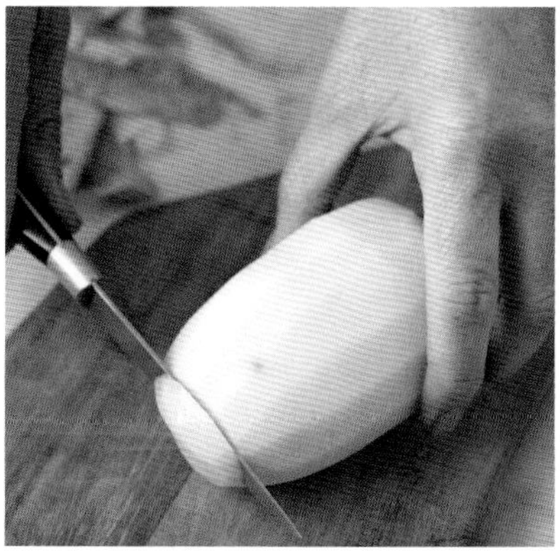

BASIC METHOD

Perfect potato chips await.

SERVES 4

PREP 30 MINS

COOK 30–40 MINS

4–5 large potatoes, peeled and cut into chips

1 tbsp vegetable oil

a couple of pinches of salt

Preheat the oven to 200°C/400°F/Gas 6. Cut your chosen potatoes into your preferred chip size and shape, place on a baking tray, toss with the oil and sprinkle with salt. Bake for 30–40 minutes until cooked and golden, turning once or twice.

FAT CHIPS

Chop your potatoes into chunky strips. Remember, they will shrink a little during cooking. You can of course leave the skins on your chips for added texture and nutrients, and less faff.

SWEET POTATO CHIPS

Cut sweet potatoes into even, medium-size strips. Since they contain quite a lot of sugar, these may burn more easily than regular potatoes, so again, keep an eye on them. You can peel them or keep the skins on.

SKINNY FRIES

Slice the potatoes into fine strips and reduce the cooking time by 10 minutes. Keep an eye on them as they may burn quickly.

FOR EXTRA FLAVOUR

Toss your fries in oil, salt and pepper, or spice them up with…

* Grated fresh garlic
* Grated vegan hard cheese
* Chilli flakes and paprika
* Pinch of curry powder
* Finely chopped fresh parsley or coriander/cilantro leaves

CLASSIC COOKED BREAKFAST

There are few more famous – or more filling – breakfasts than the 'full English'. Thankfully, there is no need to give up this traditional favourite because there are vegan versions of everything these days, 'bacon' and sausages and even 'black pudding'. No need to argue what should and shouldn't be included as you can choose what you like! This plate features a delicious tofu and corn mixture, a savoury spread on toast, and smoked tempeh, with suggestions for all sorts of other tasty additions.

SERVES 2 * PREP 20 MINS * COOK 20–25 MINS

2 tbsp vegetable oil

1 tbsp soy sauce

2 vegan sausages (see page 82 or use bought ones)

6 medium mushrooms

2 slices of smoked soya tempeh

1 large fresh tomato, halved

2 frozen potato croquettes or potato waffles

20g/¾oz fresh tofu

25g/1oz/⅓ cup frozen or canned sweetcorn

1 tsp vegan margarine

200g/7oz can of baked beans

1 tbsp soya cream cheese

1 tbsp tomato ketchup

½ tsp yeast extract

½ tsp mustard

2 slices of bread

salt and ground black pepper

TO SERVE (OPTIONAL)

orange juice or cup of tea

tomato ketchup

vegan brown sauce

mustard

1. Preheat the oven to 200°C/400°F/Gas 6. Mix the oil with the soy sauce in a cup and lightly brush it on to the sausages, mushrooms and soya tempeh slices.
2. Place the sausages on a baking tray with the tomato halves and the potato croquettes or waffles, and put into the oven.
3. When the sausages have been in the oven for 10 minutes, turn them over. Add the mushrooms and tempeh and return it all to the oven. Cook for another 10–15 minutes until everything is golden and tender.
4. Meanwhile, put the tofu and the corn in a pan with the margarine. Mix together well, and season with salt and pepper. Heat through gently, stirring frequently.
5. In a separate small pan, simmer the baked beans for about 5 minutes, until they are piping hot.
6. Mix the soya cream cheese with the tomato ketchup, yeast extract and mustard until well blended.
7. Toast the bread and spread the cream cheese and ketchup mixture evenly over both slices, then cut the slices in half diagonally.
8. Divide everything up between your plates and serve at once, with all your chosen sauces and accompaniments.

Vegan Hack

Spread some yeast extract on to your toast to sneak in some vitamin B12, sprinkle on some hemp seeds to up the omega 3 levels, and add some seaweed culinary seasoning into the scrambled tofu to boost your iodine levels.

BANGERS & MASH

Sausages and mash is a favourite comfort food, especially on a chilly evening. You can of course buy vegan sausages, but it's fun to make your own. They require a little time, but are not difficult, and you could always make a big batch and freeze some for another meal.

SERVES 4 * PREP 30 MINS + 40 MINS CHILLING * COOK 1 HR 30 MINS

1 Heat the oil in a large frying pan, add the onion and cook for 10 minutes, until soft. Add the leek, apple and thyme and cook for another 5 minutes or so until the leeks are tender. Season with salt and pepper.

2 Add the mushrooms and a little more oil if necessary, then cook for a few minutes until the mushrooms are just soft. Stir through the mustard and yeast extract.

3 Leave the mixture to cool, then spoon it into a food processor. Add the butter beans and breadcrumbs and pulse until the mixture comes together to form a fairly smooth paste. If you don't have a food processor, put everything on a large board and chop and scrape it all together until it is fairly smooth. Transfer to a bowl and chill in the fridge for 20 minutes.

4 Prepare 12 foil rectangles, each measuring about 20 × 10cm/8 × 4in. Divide the mixture between the foil pieces and roll up in the foil to make sausage shapes. Twist the ends so they are firmly sealed. Put in the fridge for another 20 minutes.

5 Pour enough water into a large pan to come about one-quarter of the way up, and sit a steamer pan or metal colander on top. Place the foil-wrapped sausages in the steamer, put a lid on and steam for about 40 minutes. Check occasionally that the water hasn't run dry – you may have to top it up with more boiling water. Remove from the heat and leave the sausages to cool for a few minutes before you unwrap the foil.

6 When you're ready to cook the sausages, preheat the oven to 200°C/400°F/Gas 6. Arrange the sausages in a roasting pan, drizzle over a little oil and cook for 30 minutes, until golden.

7 Meanwhile, make the potato mash (see method overleaf), and make up the gravy with hot water in a small pan, as per the packet instructions. To serve, spoon dollops of mash on to individual plates, with the sausages and a ladleful of gravy.

FOR THE SAUSAGES

1 tbsp vegetable oil, plus extra for cooking the sausages

1 onion, peeled and finely chopped

1 leek, trimmed and finely chopped

1 cooking apple, peeled, cored and chopped

a small bunch of thyme, leaves only

400g/14oz white mushrooms, finely chopped

2 tsp Dijon mustard

1 tsp yeast extract

400g/14oz can of butter beans, drained

100g/3¾oz/1⅔ cups fine fresh breadcrumbs

salt and ground black pepper

TO SERVE

4–5 potatoes, 3 tbsp vegan margarine and 3–4 tbsp vegan milk for classic potato mash (see page 85)

vegan gravy granules

BEETROOT MASH
SWEET POTATO MASH
PESTO & PEA MASH

MASH MANIA

Classic creamy potato mash is always good, but why not try mixing things up for a change – other delicious mash ideas are offered below.

POTATO MASH

Creamy potato mash goes with everything (especially sausages and gravy, see previous page) but the method works well for other vegetable mashes too.

SERVES 4

PREP 20 MINS

COOK 30 MINS

4–5 large potatoes, peeled and cut into even-size pieces

3 tbsp vegan margarine

3–4 tbsp vegan milk

salt and ground black pepper

1 Boil the potatoes in a large pan of salted water, with the lid ajar, for about 20 minutes, until tender when you poke them with a knife. Drain well, then tip them back into the pan.

2 Put the lid on and sit them back on the unlit hob (turn off the heat source) to steam-dry for 5 minutes.

3 Remove the lid and let the steam clear, then add the margarine and mash really well to remove any lumps. Pour in the milk and add the seasoning, then mash again until really creamy. Taste and adjust the seasoning as needed.

BEETROOT MASH

Make the mashed potato as described above. While the potatoes are cooking, blend 3 balls of ready-cooked beetroot in a food processor and then combine the purée with the potato for a lovely deep pink mash.

SWEET POTATO MASH

Put 4 peeled and quartered sweet potatoes in a pan of salted boiling water and boil for 15–20 minutes, until tender. Drain well, leave to steam-dry for a few minutes, then mash with 3 tbsp vegan margarine until smooth. Season to taste. You probably won't need any milk, but do feel free to add some if you want runnier mash.

PESTO & PEA MASH

Make the mashed potato as described above, then stir in 3 tbsp vegan pesto and 115g/4oz/1 cup cooked and lightly mashed peas.

CORN ON THE COB

Served just on its own as a tasty treat or alongside burgers or kebabs at a barbecue, corn is always popular, and so easy to prepare. Here, the sweet, tender cobs are taken to the next level by the addition of flavoured butters. If possible, try to find a product labelled as vegan butter rather than regular vegan margarine for this particular recipe, as it will taste better.

SERVES 4 * PREP 15 MINS + 30 MINS CHILLING * COOK 5 MINS

1. First, make whichever flavoured butter you want to use (or all of them!). Simply put the butter in a bowl along with the flavourings and beat until combined.

2. Scrape the butter on to a piece of clear film or plastic wrap in a long sausage shape, fold over the film to cover, then using the flat of your hand, roll it into a log shape. Twist the ends of the film until tight. Put the log in the fridge for 30 minutes or overnight to chill and firm up.

3. When you're ready to cook, put the corn cobs in a large pan of boiling salted water and cook for about 5 minutes, until tender. Remove very carefully using tongs and transfer to serving plates.

4. While the corn is boiling, slice off as many rounds from the butter log as you need. Put these on top of the hot corn on the plates and enjoy. Napkins are recommended…

GET GRIDDLING!

Corn on the cob works brilliantly on the barbecue. Place the cobs on pieces of foil, smother with the flavoured butter, then wrap fairly tightly, twisting the ends so the butter can't escape. Place the cobs on the barbecue and cook for 15 minutes. Remove the cobs from the foil and brush with more butter, then griddle for a further 5 minutes, until golden and beginning to blacken.

4 corn on the cob

FOR THE CHILLI & LIME BUTTER

115g/4oz/½ cup vegan butter

1 fresh red chilli, seeded and finely chopped (use less if you don't want it too hot)

zest of ½ lime

FOR THE HERBY BUTTER

115g/4oz/½ cup vegan butter

a small bunch of flat leaf parsley, finely chopped

FOR THE TEX-MEX BUTTER

115g/4oz/½ cup vegan butter

1 garlic clove, peeled and grated

1 tsp fresh coriander/cilantro leaves, finely chopped

½ tsp chilli powder

¼ tsp ground cumin

1 tsp ground paprika

juice of 1 lime

TOFU KEBABS WITH MAPLE & PINEAPPLE GLAZE

This is an exciting way to eat your veg. Serve the kebabs on their own or with a big colourful salad and crusty bread. Here, they are cooked in the oven for ease, but you could always fire up the barbecue or cook them under the grill or broiler for a smoky, charred flavour.

SERVES 4 * PREP 15 MINS + 20 MINS SOAKING * COOK 30 MINS

1 Soak some wooden skewers in cold water for 20 minutes. Preheat the oven to 200°C/400°F/Gas 6.

2 To make the glaze, mix together the maple syrup, pineapple juice and soy sauce, and season with salt and pepper. Put to one side

3 Thread the tofu, tomatoes and peppers alternately on to the soaked wooden skewers and brush liberally with the glaze. Place the skewers on a griddle pan or in a large baking dish.

4 Put in the oven and cook for about 30 minutes, or until golden brown, brushing with more glaze halfway through cooking. Remove from oven and serve.

COOK'S NOTES

* Try to cut all the veg and tofu into similar-sized pieces, so everything cooks evenly.

* You can skewer lots of other things … red onions, courgettes/zucchini, aubergine/eggplant, mushrooms and even whole mild chillies if you like!

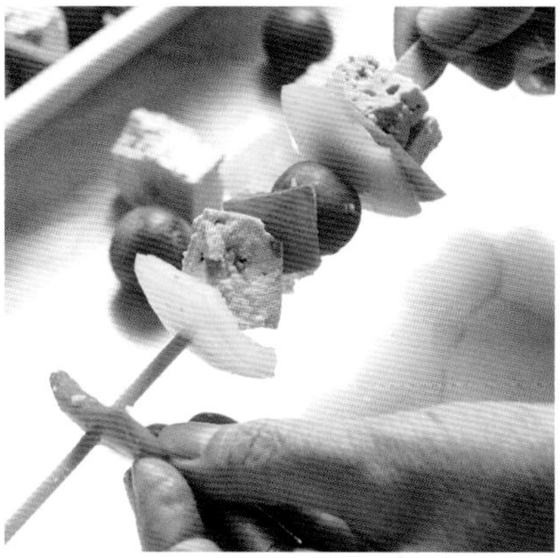

375g/13oz firm tofu, pressed to remove the water and cut into chunky cubes

250g/9oz cherry tomatoes

2 yellow bell peppers, halved, seeded and chopped into chunky pieces

2 red bell peppers, halved, seeded and chopped into chunky pieces

FOR THE GLAZE

4 tbsp maple syrup

4 tbsp pineapple juice

2 tbsp soy sauce

salt and ground black pepper

VEG TEMPURA WITH SOY DIPPING SAUCE

These lightly battered deep-fried vegetables are the tastiest way to eat your five a day. The secret to the perfect batter is to use fizzy water, which makes it nice and light.

SERVES 4 * PREP 20 MINS * COOK 10 MINS

1. First, make the batter. Put the cornflour and flour in a large bowl, whisk to combine, then make a dip in the middle. Slowly pour in the sparking water, whisking all the time, until the batter is smooth. Put to one side.

2. For the dipping sauce, mix together all the ingredients in a bowl and put to one side. Place some sheets of kitchen paper on a plate.

3. Pour the vegetable oil into a wok or suitable pan for deep-frying so it comes about one-third of the way up the sides. (If you aren't an adult, ask one to help with this deep-frying stage.) Heat the oil until it is really hot – if you drop a small trickle of the batter in the oil it should sizzle and rise to the surface within a few seconds, or you can test the temperature with a thermometer and check it reads 180°C/375°F.

4. When the oil is ready, dip the vegetable pieces into the batter one by one, so it just coats them, then carefully lay them in the hot oil and fry for about 2 minutes, until they are golden and rise to the surface. Do not crowd the pan.

5. Remove the veg with a slotted spoon once they are done and place them on the kitchen paper to drain. Continue until all the vegetables are cooked. Serve with the dip.

COOK'S NOTES

* Use a deep-fat fryer for this if you have one.
* If you don't fancy bell peppers or broccoli, you can use all kinds of other veggies. Good alternatives are chunks of courgette/zucchini or aubergine/eggplant, cauliflower florets, slices of sweet potato, or whole or halved mushrooms.

1 head of broccoli, broken into florets

2 red and 2 yellow bell peppers, halved, seeded and roughly chopped

vegetable oil, for frying

FOR THE BATTER

75g/3oz/⅔ cup cornflour/cornstarch

25g/1oz/¼ cup plain/all-purpose flour

100ml/3½fl oz/½ cup cold sparkling water

FOR THE DIPPING SAUCE

4 tbsp soy sauce

1 tbsp rice vinegar

½ tbsp water

1 tsp maple syrup

SWEETCORN & SPRING ONION FRITTERS

Fritters are loved by everyone and they are so simple to make – perfect for a quick lunch with a salad or eaten cold on the go. They're also really easy to adapt using whatever veg you have to hand; just make sure the vegetables are small or finely chopped.

SERVES 4 * PREP 20 MINS * COOK 30–40 MINS

340g/11½oz can of sweetcorn, drained

liquid from a 400g/14oz can of chickpeas/garbanzos

a bunch of spring onions/scallions, trimmed and finely chopped

1 tbsp flaxseeds mixed with 1 tbsp water

2 tbsp plain/all-purpose flour

1–2 tbsp vegetable oil

salt and ground black pepper

1. Put all the ingredients except the oil in a bowl and mix well until combined. If the mixture is too thin, stir in a little more flour and if it is too thick, add a little water to loosen it. It should just drop off the spoon.

2. Heat a drizzle of the oil in a heavy non-stick frying pan or skillet. When it is hot, put a large dollop of the mixture in the pan (for a perfect round, sit a metal pastry cutter in the pan and spoon the mixture into that) and cook for 3–4 minutes or until the underside is beginning to turn golden. If using, carefully remove the cutter, then flip over the fritter using a large spatula.

3. Cook the other side for a further few minutes, until it is golden brown. Remove to a plate lined with kitchen paper to drain, and keep warm.

4. Continue cooking the rest of the mixture in the same way, adding a little more oil as you need it. Stack the fritters and serve hot or cold.

COOK'S NOTE

Depending on the size of your pan, you may be able to fry several fritters at once, which will cut down on the cooking time.

COURGETTE & 'CHEESE' FRITTERS

Here, juicy courgettes and vegan Greek-style cheese are added to a thick batter made with vegan milk and flavoured with spring onions and fresh mint, and then pan-fried in big spoonfuls to make tasty fritters. Enjoy as a light lunch, snack or accompaniment.

SERVES 4 * PREP 20 MINS * COOK 30 MINS

450g/1lb courgettes/zucchini

2 tbsp vegetable oil, plus extra for frying

6 spring onions/scallions, trimmed and finely chopped

25g/1oz/¼ cup chickpea/gram flour

2 tbsp cornflour/cornstarch

3 tbsp vegan milk

a small bunch of fresh mint, leaves finely chopped

150g/5oz vegan feta-style cheese, finely chopped or crumbled

ground black pepper

green salad, to serve (optional)

1. Lay a clean dish towel on the work surface and grate the courgettes on to it. Gather up the corners of the towel, then use your hands to squeeze the excess liquid out over the sink.
2. Heat the 2 tbsp of oil in a heavy non-stick frying pan or skillet and gently fry the spring onions for 3–4 minutes, until soft. Transfer to a large bowl.
3. In a separate bowl, blend the chickpea flour, cornflour and milk together. Season with pepper and add the spring onions, courgette and mint.
4. Stir everything together (the batter will seem quite thick at first, but moisture from the courgettes will loosen it), then stir in the crumbled cheese. Let the batter stand for 3–4 minutes, then stir again.
5. Add a little more oil to the frying pan and place over a medium heat. When hot, drop large spoonfuls of the fritter batter into the pan – make 3 or 4 fritters at a time – and cook for 3–4 minutes, or until set and lightly browned, then turn over and cook the other side for 3–4 minutes, or until browned.
6. Drain the fritters on kitchen paper and keep them warm while you cook the remaining mixture in the same way. You may need a splash more oil. Serve warm, with a green salad if you wish.

VARIATION

Instead of mint, flavour the fritters with chopped fresh coriander/cilantro and a fresh red chilli, seeded and finely chopped.

COCONUT PATTIES

These originally hail from India, where they are made from grated fresh coconut. Use this if you have time, but for simplicity, here they are made with desiccated coconut softened with coconut water.

MAKES 16 * PREP 20 MINS + 10 MINS SOAKING * COOK 30 MINS

1. Put the coconut in a large bowl and pour over the warm coconut water. Set aside for 10 minutes for the coconut to absorb the water. Cut the bread into small pieces.
2. Place all the ingredients, except the onion and the oil, in a food processor and blitz to a smooth paste. If you don't have a food processor, put everything on your largest board and chop it all together with a large knife, scraping and blending it as you go.
3. Transfer the mixture to a bowl and add the onion. Mix thoroughly and divide the mixture into 16 balls, each the size of a lime.
4. Flatten the coconut balls to form smooth, round patties. If the mixture sticks to your fingers, moisten your palms with water between patties.
5. Put 1 tbsp of the coconut oil in a non-stick frying pan and heat over a medium-high heat. Fry the patties in batches for 3–4 minutes on each side, until browned all over.
6. Lift out and drain on kitchen paper. Keep warm while you fry the other patties, adding more oil to the pan when necessary. Serve immediately with the chutney.

150g/5oz/2 cups desiccated/dry unsweetened shredded coconut

150ml/¼ pint/⅔ cup coconut water, warmed

2 slices of bread, crusts removed

75g/3oz/⅔ cup chickpea/gram flour

1–2 fresh green chillies, seeded and roughly chopped

2.5cm/1in piece of fresh root ginger, peeled and roughly chopped

1 large garlic clove, peeled and roughly chopped

1 tbsp chopped fresh coriander/cilantro leaves and stalks

½ tsp chilli powder, or to taste

½ tsp salt, or to taste

1 medium onion, peeled and finely chopped

coconut oil, for shallow-frying

chutney, to serve

TOFU HOISIN HOT PITTA

This is the easiest throw-together meal and it will really satisfy both the body and the tastebuds – it's salty and sweet, and packed with protein and carbs!

MAKES 4 * PREP 10 MINS + 10 MINS SOAKING * COOK 10 MINS

1. Put the onion in a small bowl, cover with cold water and leave it to soak for 10 minutes before draining. This removes some of the astringency from the raw onion.

2. Heat the oil in a large frying pan, then add the marinated tofu and about half the hoisin sauce. Toss it around the pan so it all gets coated and cook, stirring occasionally, for about 10 minutes. Remove and put to one side.

3. Fill each of the warmed breads with a little remaining hoisin sauce, then stuff with lettuce, tomatoes, onion and tofu and enjoy.

½ red onion, peeled and finely sliced

1 tbsp vegetable oil

375g/13oz ready-marinated tofu cubes

about 4 tbsp hoisin sauce

a handful of crisp lettuce, such as cos or romaine, roughly chopped

4 tomatoes, sliced

4 large pitta or flatbreads, warmed

Look Out!

Check the label on the pitta or flatbread packet – just to make sure there is no added dairy milk.

PULLED JACKFRUIT WRAPS

Not only is jackfruit delicious and incredibly versatile, but it is also an excellent source of B-vitamins and is full of dietary fibre. These tasty wraps will keep you going right through until supper.

MAKES 4 * PREP 10 MINS + 10 MINS SOAKING * COOK 6–8 MINS

½ red onion, peeled and finely sliced
1 tbsp dark soy sauce
juice of ½ lime, the remaining ½ cut into fine wedges for serving
5cm/2in piece of fresh root ginger, peeled and finely grated
a pinch of chilli flakes
565g/20oz can of young jackfruit, drained and roughly shredded
½ tbsp vegetable oil
4 large wholemeal wraps, warmed
a large handful of salad leaves
2 avocados, halved, stoned and sliced

1. Put the onion in a small bowl, cover with cold water and leave it to soak for 10 minutes before draining. This removes some of the astringency from the raw onion.
2. Put the soy sauce, lime juice, ginger and chilli flakes in a large bowl, add the jackfruit and toss to coat.
3. Heat the oil in a pan and add the jackfruit mixture, then cook and stir around the pan for 4–5 minutes. Let it bubble a little and cook for a few minutes more. Remove from the heat and stir through the drained onion.
4. Divide the mixture up between the wraps along with the salad leaves and avocado, then fold or roll and serve with a few lime wedges.

COOK'S NOTE

Canned jackfruit is often packed with water and sometimes some salt so it is a good idea to rinse it in cold water and drain it.

Vegan Hack

In recent years, jackfruit has been hailed as a vegetarian meat alternative as it isn't as processed as other vegan 'meats', and when shredded the texture resembles that of pulled chicken or pulled pork. However, it is relatively low in protein so shouldn't be used as a regular protein source. Its high number of B vitamins and fibre will keep you fuller for longer though, and support your metabolism, blood health and heart.

CHINESE PANCAKES WITH SHREDDED MOCK DUCK

All the excitement of a Chinese takeaway in hardly any more time than it takes to place your order. This recipe couldn't be simpler – you just heat up some mock duck and serve it with the pancakes and accompaniments – but it really packs a punch in the flavour stakes and is great for sharing with friends.

MAKES 12 * **PREP 5 MINS** * **COOK 6 MINS**

1 Heat the oil in a large frying pan, add the shredded 'duck' and cook for about 6 minutes or as per the packet instructions. Transfer to a serving dish.

2 Heat the Chinese pancakes in the microwave for about 30 seconds or as per packet instructions and transfer to a serving plate or board. Place everything on the table.

3 To assemble, spread a pancake with a little of the sauce, spoon some shredded 'duck' down the middle and top with spring onion and cucumber. Roll the pancake up and dip it in more of the sauce as you eat, if you like.

1 tbsp vegetable oil

300g/11oz vegan shredded hoisin 'duck'

12 Chinese pancakes

plum sauce or hoisin sauce

a bunch of spring onions/scallions, trimmed and finely sliced lengthways

1 cucumber, halved lengthways, seeds scooped out and sliced into fine strips

CHEESE & TOMATO QUESADILLAS

This easy-to-prepare snack is a great vegan alternative to cheese toasties. There are many variations, but in this one, vegan cheese that melts is combined with chopped tomatoes, chilli and fresh coriander. Vary the filling depending on the ingredients in your fridge.

MAKES 4 * PREP 5 MINS * COOK 15 MINS

1. Sprinkle the cheese over 4 of the tortillas, dividing it up equally. Mix together the tomato, chilli, fresh coriander and a little salt and pepper.
2. Scatter the tomato mixture over the cheese, then top with the remaining tortillas, firmly pressing the pairs together.
3. Lightly brush a ridged griddle pan, heavy frying pan or skillet with a little oil. Cook the tortillas one at a time in the pan for 1½–2 minutes on each side, carefully turning them with a wide spatula, until the cheese has begun to melt and the tortillas are crisp. Brush the pan with a little more oil before cooking the next one.
4. Serve the stuffed tortillas immediately, while they are still hot.

225g/8oz/2 cups vegan mozzarella-style or Cheddar-style cheese, grated

8 flour tortillas

4 tomatoes, chopped

1 fresh chilli, seeded and chopped

½ bunch of fresh coriander/cilantro leaves, roughly chopped

salt and ground black pepper

vegetable oil, for brushing

SAUSAGE, MUSHROOM & CHEESE TOASTIES

Toasties are a quick-fix meal for any time of the day, and are incredibly versatile. These ones are like a cooked breakfast in open sandwich form, with the added bonus of some oozingly melted cheese to bring the whole thing together. If you want to make your own vegan sausages, turn to page 82.

MAKES 4 * PREP 10 MINS * COOK 25 MINS

4–6 vegan sausages

about 1 tbsp vegetable or olive oil

200g/7oz mushrooms, sliced

4 slices of sourdough bread or similar

50g/2oz/⅔ cup vegan Cheddar-style cheese, grated

salt and ground black pepper

1. Preheat the oven to 200°C/400°F/Gas 6. Put the sausages in a roasting pan, drizzle with a little oil, and cook in the oven for about 20 minutes until golden. Remove and keep warm, then slice the sausages lengthways.

2. Heat the remaining oil in a frying pan and add the mushrooms. Season with salt and pepper and fry for a couple of minutes, until golden.

3. Lightly brush the bread slices with oil, and toast on a heavy griddle until golden and crisp, turning once. You can also use a toaster, without brushing with oil.

4. Top the toasts with the sausage and mushrooms, sprinkle over the cheese and put in the oven for a couple of minutes, until the cheese has melted. Serve.

Vegan Hack

If you have an excess of vegan cheese, you can wrap it in one block and store it in the freezer, or grate it and freeze it in portions. It will freeze for up to 3 months. For cooking, you can use it straight from the freezer, but if you want to eat it in its non-melted form, let it defrost first.

ALMOST EGG & CRESS PINWHEELS PAGE 110
'VLT' PAGE 109
BEAN & PESTO PASTE WITH CARROT PAGE 111

SANDWICHES 3 WAYS

This trio of sandwich suggestions offer fillings that you may feel you are missing out on by being vegan, which are not only tasty but also really healthy, packed with all sorts of nutritious ingredients that will help you stay full for ages.

THE 'VLT'

This vegan version of the BLT (Vegan Bacon, Lettuce & Tomato) hits the spot whenever you're feeling a bit peckish. The bacon is replaced with vegan bacon slices, but you could also use fried slices of smoked soya tempeh, as described in the cooked breakfast on page 80.

SERVES 2 * PREP 15 MINS * COOK 15 MINS

1. Preheat the oven to 200°C/400°F/Gas 6. Put the vegan 'bacon' slices on a baking sheet, drizzle with the oil and put in the oven to cook for about 15 minutes or until crisp. Remove and put to one side.

2. To assemble, layer up the bread or rolls with lettuce, tomato, 'bacon' and mayonnaise.

5–6 vegan 'bacon' slices
a drizzle of vegetable oil
white or brown sliced bread or rolls
a handful of crisp lettuce leaves
2 tomatoes, sliced
2 tbsp vegan mayonnaise

ALMOST EGG & CRESS SANDWICHES

Made with crushed chickpeas flavoured with capers and lemon and bound with vegan mayo, this vibrant filling is quick to put together and keeps well for a few days in the fridge if you want to make up a batch. Roll up in tortillas for the pretty pinwheel wraps on page 108.

SERVES 2–4 * PREP 15 MINS

1. Put the chickpeas in a food processor along with the turmeric, capers, lemon juice and seasoning. Whiz until combined, but leave some texture in it. Taste and adjust as necessary, adding more salt or lemon juice. If you don't have a food processor, put everything on your largest board and chop it all together with a large knife, scraping and blending as you go.

2. Transfer the mixture to a bowl and stir in the vegan mayonnaise.

3. Spread the filling on your chosen bread to make sandwiches, topping with celery and cress if using, and sandwich together. If using tortilla wraps, spread the filling mixture over the wrap, roll and slice into pinwheels to serve.

- 400g/14oz can of chickpeas/garbanzos, drained (you could reserve the liquid aquafaba for another recipe)
- 1 tsp ground turmeric
- 1 tbsp capers, chopped
- 1 tsp lemon juice
- 2–3 tbsp vegan mayonnaise
- sliced white or brown bread, rolls, pitta pockets or tortilla wraps
- 2 celery sticks, finely sliced (optional)
- garden cress (optional)
- salt and ground black pepper

BEAN & PESTO PASTE WITH CARROT

This is a power sarni, packed with a hummus-type paste made with protein-packed beans and tasty pesto combined with grated carrots. It is quite a moist mixture, so it could make your sandwiches soggy if you make it too far in advance; it's best to serve it immediately if possible.

SERVES 4 * PREP 20 MINS

1. Put the beans, tomato pesto, salt and pepper in a food processor and whiz until a smooth paste forms. If you don't have a food processor, put everything on your largest board and chop it all together with a large knife, scraping and blending it as you go.

2. Spread the filling on your chosen bread, top with the grated carrot and cucumber slices and sandwich together. If using pittas, fill and slice, or spread over tortilla wraps, fold or roll up and maybe slice into pinwheels.

400g/14oz can of cannellini beans or butter/lima beans, drained

3–4 tbsp vegan sun-dried tomato pesto

sliced white or brown bread, rolls, pitta pocket or tortilla wraps

1–2 carrots, peeled and grated

¼ cucumber, finely sliced

salt and ground black pepper

BAKES ROASTS & ONE-POTS

CHESTNUT ROAST...

Stick with tradition on a Sunday and don't miss out on the roast dinner. This is a truly delicious chestnut loaf that will have everyone asking for an extra slice. Serve up platefuls with your favourite roasted vegetables and cauli cheese (all described overleaf), vegan sausages, and lashings of vegan gravy.

SERVES 4 * PREP 1 HR * COOK 50 MINS

1. Preheat the oven to 180°C/350°F/Gas 4 and lightly grease a loaf tin/pan measuring about 20 × 20cm/8 × 8in.
2. Heat the oil in a large frying pan, add the onion, season with salt and pepper and cook for 10 minutes, until the onion is soft. Put the chestnuts or mixed nuts in a food processor and whiz until ground, leaving a bit of texture. Alternatively, you could do this on a large board with a knife.
3. Add the thyme to the onions and cook for a minute, then remove from the heat. Stir in the nut mixture, the breadcrumbs, milk and flour, then transfer to the greased tin.
4. Put the nut roast in the oven and bake for about 40 minutes or until golden and firm.
5. While the nut roast is baking, prepare the potatoes and vegetables at the same time, to serve together for a roast dinner with all the trimmings (see overleaf).

1 tbsp vegetable oil

1 red onion, peeled and finely chopped

200g/7oz chestnuts (from a vacuum pack) or unsalted mixed nuts

a few thyme stalks, leaves only, chopped

125g/4$\frac{1}{4}$oz/2$\frac{1}{4}$ cups fresh breadcrumbs

150ml/$\frac{1}{4}$ pint/$\frac{2}{3}$ cup vegan milk

1 tbsp plain/all-purpose flour

salt and ground black pepper

... WITH ALL THE TRIMMINGS

While you are making your chestnut roast on the previous page, here's how to prepare the wonderful accompaniments that make up a roast dinner. To make life easier, you could make the nut roast and cauliflower cheese in advance, then just reheat them in the microwave when you're ready. Mix and match your favourite vegetables.

SERVES 4 * **PREP 1 HR** * **COOK 50 MINS**

8–12 vegan sausages (see page 80 or use bought ones)

5 carrots, peeled and cut into rounds

1 head of broccoli, cut into florets

salt and ground black pepper

vegan gravy granules

FOR THE ROASTED POTATOES AND PARSNIPS

900g/2lb potatoes, peeled and quartered or cut into even-sized pieces

1 tbsp plain/all-purpose flour

4 tbsp vegetable oil

6 parsnips, peeled and sliced lengthways

salt and ground black pepper

FOR THE CAULIFLOWER CHEESE

1 head of cauliflower, cut into florets

100g/3¾oz/8 tbsp vegan margarine

1 tbsp plain/all-purpose flour

300ml/½ pint/1¼ cups vegan milk

2 tsp Dijon mustard

150g/5oz/1¼ cups vegan Cheddar-style cheese, grated

salt and ground black pepper

1. Heat the oven to 180°C/350°F/Gas 4. Boil the potatoes in a pan of salted boiling water for 6–8 minutes, until a little tender. Do not overcook. Drain well, tip the potatoes back into the pan, add the flour, put the lid on the pan and shake so the potatoes get covered in flour and the edges are roughed up. This will help you to make really good crispy roast potatoes.

2. Put 3 tbsp of the oil in a large roasting pan and put in the oven for 5 minutes, until it gets really hot. Remove the pan from the oven and toss the potatoes in the hot oil, being careful it doesn't splash. (If you are not one, ask an adult to help.) Season with salt and pepper and put back in the oven for about 40 minutes, until the potatoes are golden and crisp. The potatoes can go into the oven at the same time as the nut roast.

3. Put the parsnips in another roasting pan and toss with the remaining 1 tbsp oil, season with salt and pepper, and put them in the oven 10 minutes after the potatoes; the parsnips will need to cook for about 30 minutes, until crisp and golden.

4. Cook the cauliflower in a pan of salted water for 10–15 minutes, until just tender. Drain well and transfer to an ovenproof dish. Melt the margarine in a pan, then stir in the flour to form a paste. Cook, stirring, for 1 minute. Add the milk a little at a time, whisking continuously so the sauce is smooth. Whisk in the mustard and vegan cheese. Taste and season if it needs it, then pour the cheese sauce over the cauliflower and put it in the oven for about 20 minutes, until golden.

5. Meanwhile, since the oven will be full, pan-fry the sausages for about 20 minutes or as packet instructions.

6. Boil the carrots and broccoli in a pan of salted water for about 6 minutes until tender, then drain and keep warm. Make the gravy as per packet instructions, stirring until it is smooth. Now you can serve it all up!

VEGAN TOAD IN THE HOLE

The vegan batter might not rise up quite as much as a traditional egg batter but it is still super-tasty and relatively easy to make. To accompany this bake you could serve up mashed potato, cooked vegetables and vegan gravy.

SERVES 4 * PREP 15 MINS + 30 MINS RESTING * COOK 45 MINS

1. Put the flour and baking powder in a large bowl, whisk to combine, then make a dip in the middle. Pour in the milk and aquafaba and whisk until combined and smooth. Transfer the batter to a jug or pitcher and put in the fridge for 30 minutes to rest.
2. Meanwhile, preheat the oven to 200°C/400°F/Gas 6. Put the oil in a roasting pan and add the sausages. Cook for about 15 minutes, then remove from the oven (be careful, the oil will be very hot and may spit).
3. Give the batter a quick stir, then pour it over the hot oil and sausages. Return the roasting pan to the oven.
4. Leave to cook for 25–30 minutes, until risen and golden brown. Serve hot.

VARIATION

You can make toad in the hole in one large dish, as here, or several individual ones. To make individual portions, cut the sausages in half and divide between an 8-hole muffin tin/pan. Add a little oil to each and put in the oven for about 10 minutes to cook; when they are browned, carefully remove the tin from the oven (ask an adult to help if necessary), and pour in enough batter to half fill each hole. Cook for 20–25 minutes, until risen and golden.

150g/5oz/1¼ cups self-raising/self-rising flour

1 tsp baking powder

300ml/½ pint/1¼ cups vegan milk

50ml/2fl oz/¼ cup aquafaba i.e. liquid from a can of chickpeas/garbanzos

2 tbsp vegetable oil

8 vegan sausages (see page 80 or use bought ones)

salt and ground black pepper

CAJUN TRAY BAKE

This traybake is simplicity itself to put together, leaving you free to do other things while it does its stuff in the oven. Here, we've used a delicious mixture of veggie 'chicken' pieces combined with potatoes, corn, peppers and tomatoes, but you could swap in other veg as you like, so long as they are cut into similar-size chunks.

SERVES 4 * PREP 20 MINS * COOK 30 MINS

1. Preheat the oven to 200°C/400°F/Gas 6. To make the Cajun spice rub, mix all the herb and spice ingredients together in a small bowl.

2. Put the 'chicken' pieces, potatoes, corn cob slices, tomatoes and chopped peppers in a roasting pan, sprinkle over the spice rub and drizzle over the oil. Now get your hands in and toss everything together until it is really well coated.

3. Put in the oven to cook for about 30 minutes, until the potatoes and corn are tender. Squeeze over lemon or lime juice and serve with tortilla triangles and some sour cream on the side.

COOK'S NOTES

* Garlic powder and onion powder are extremely useful for instantly adding flavour, but use them sparingly as they pack a real punch.

* Make this as hot as you like. The heat is in the cayenne pepper, so omit it, or add more, as you like.

Look Out!

You may be able to find other vegan 'chicken' chunks or cutlets, but always read the label as they may be veggie but not vegan, as some do contain egg.

275g/10oz vegan 'chicken' pieces

400g/14oz new potatoes, larger ones halved

2 corn on the cob, chopped into thick rounds

a handful of cherry tomatoes

2 red or orange bell peppers, halved, seeded and roughly chopped

2 tbsp vegetable oil

½ lemon or lime, for squeezing over

8 warm tortilla wraps, cut into wedges, and vegan sour cream, to serve

FOR THE CAJUN SPICE RUB

1 tsp paprika

1 tsp garlic powder

1 tsp onion powder

1 tsp dried oregano

¼ tsp salt

¼ tsp ground black pepper

¼ tsp cayenne pepper

a few thyme stalks, leaves only, finely chopped

CHEESY NACHOS BAKE WITH GUACAMOLE

Whether you are watching the match or a family movie on TV, a Mexican-style all-in-one traybake of cheesy nachos is perfect for sharing, and it's easy to prepare the elements ahead. You could also serve the bean mash, salsa and guacamole separately as dips for cheesy-baked tortilla chips.

SERVES 4–6 * PREP 20 MINS * COOK 5 MINS

1. Preheat the oven to 190°C/375°F/Gas 5. Tip the tortilla chips into a large baking pan and spread out evenly.

2. For the spiced bean mash, drain the black beans but do not rinse them, tip into a bowl and add the garlic, chilli powder and cumin. Season with a little salt (don't use too much as the tortilla chips are already salty) and pepper, then roughly mash with a fork. Mix in about 2 tbsp cold water or enough to make a creamy mash. Set aside.

3. For the tomato salsa, whisk the olive oil and lime juice together in a bowl, then stir in the chopped onion and tomato. Keep a few leaves for garnish then chop a handful of fresh coriander finely and stir into the salsa. Set aside.

4. For the guacamole, first halve the avocados, remove the stones and chop the flesh. Put the chopped avocado in a bowl, sprinkle over the lime juice and roughly mash with a fork, keeping some texture. Stir in the chopped spring onions and Tabasco sauce, if using. Spoon into a serving bowl and set aside.

5. Spoon the bean mash in little mounds all over the tortilla chips, then, using a draining spoon so that the juices are left behind, spoon over the tomato salsa. Scatter over the chilli strips if using, and grated cheese.

6. Bake for about 5 minutes, until everything is hot, but take care not to over-brown the tortilla chips. Remove the pan from the oven.

7. Spoon over blobs of the sour cream and scatter with the reserved fresh coriander leaves. Serve on small plates with a scoop of the guacamole dolloped on top.

200g/7oz corn tortilla chips

1 green seeded chilli, sliced (optional)

115g/4oz/1 cup vegan mozzarella-style cheese, grated

2 tbsp vegan sour cream

FOR THE BEAN MASH

400g/14oz can of black beans

1 garlic clove, peeled and crushed

½ tsp mild chilli powder

¼ tsp ground cumin

salt and ground black pepper

FOR THE TOMATO SALSA

1 tbsp olive oil

1 tbsp lime juice

¼ red onion, peeled and chopped

6 tomatoes, skinned, seeded and diced

a bunch of fresh coriander/cilantro

FOR THE GUACAMOLE

2 ripe avocados

1 tbsp lime juice

2 spring onions/scallions, chopped

2–3 drops of Tabasco sauce (optional)

ROAST VEGETABLE TIKKA

This is the ultimate in lazy curry-making since everything is thrown into a roasting pan, coated in a ready-made curry paste and the oven does the rest of the work! This recipe just uses vegetables with some added chickpeas for protein, but you could add cubes of tofu or tempeh or vegan 'chicken' pieces, if you like.

SERVES 4–6 * PREP 20 MINS * COOK 30–40 MINS

1 fresh red chilli, seeded and finely chopped (optional)

3 tsp mild curry powder

1 tbsp tomato paste

2 tbsp vegetable oil

1 head of cauliflower, cut into florets

1 butternut squash, halved, peeled, seeded and cut into wedges

1 head of broccoli, cut into florets

200g/7oz green beans

8–12 cherry tomatoes

400g/14oz can of chickpeas/garbanzos, drained (you could reserve the liquid aquafaba for another recipe)

salt and ground black pepper

vegan naan breads, mango chutney, and a mint vegan yogurt dip, to serve (optional)

1. Preheat the oven to 200°C/400°F/Gas 6. Mix the chilli, curry powder, tomato paste, oil and seasoning together in a small bowl.
2. Put the cauliflower, squash, broccoli, green beans and tomatoes in a large roasting pan.
3. Pour the spice paste over the vegetables and, using your hands if easier, toss it all together so everything gets well coated. Put in the oven and roast for 30–40 minutes or until it is all charred and tender.
4. Add the drained chickpeas for the last 10 minutes of cooking time.
5. Serve with naan breads, mango chutney and mint yogurt on the side, as you like.

Minty Yogurt

For a fresh raita-style dip mix 250ml/8fl oz vegan Greek-style plain yogurt with a handful of finely chopped fresh mint leaves.

SAMOSAS

These crisp triangles of filo pastry are filled with a spicy lentil and potato mix. Filo pastry is usually always vegan but do check the label to be sure. These can be eaten hot or cold, on their own, with chutney, or with a salad

MAKES 16–20 * PREP 30 MINS + COOLING * COOK 1 HR

1. Put the potatoes in a pan of salted boiling water and boil for about 5 minutes, until tender, but don't let them get too soft. Drain well and put to one side.

2. Meanwhile, heat the oil in a large frying pan, add the onion, season with salt and pepper and cook for 10 minutes, until the onion is soft.

3. Stir in the lentils and spices and cook for a few more minutes. Add the peas and stock, bring to the boil, then reduce to a simmer and cook gently for 15–20 minutes or until the stock is almost absorbed.

4. Stir through the potatoes, taste and season a little more if it needs it. Put the mixture to one side and let it cool.

5. Preheat the oven to 200°C/400°F/Gas 6. Cut the sheets of filo in half lengthways – each piece should be about 15 × 33cm/6 × 13in. Brush each piece with melted margarine as you go, and stack the strips in neat pairs.

6. Spoon 1–2 tbsp of the filling mixture into the top centre of each piece of pastry, not too close to the edge, and form it into a triangle shape. Bring over the top corner of pastry to cover the mixture, forming a triangle, then continue folding the pastry like this to the bottom of the pastry strip. Repeat with the remaining filling and pastry. (If you have too much filling, the leftover mixture could be put in an airtight container to use another day – it's delicious served warm with some naan.)

7. Place the triangles on a baking sheet, folded edge down, and sprinkle with sesame seeds, if using. Put in the oven and bake for 20–30 minutes, until golden and crisp.

8. Remove from the oven and transfer to a wire rack to cool a little. These samosas can be eaten hot or cold.

3 medium potatoes, peeled and cut into small cubes

1 tbsp vegetable oil

1 onion, peeled and finely chopped

2 × 400g/14oz cans of brown or green lentils, drained

2 tsp garam masala

1 tsp mild curry powder

200g/7oz/1¾ cups frozen peas, defrosted

about 400ml/14fl oz/1⅔ cups hot vegetable stock

400g/14oz filo pastry

150g/5oz/¾ cup vegan margarine, melted

1 tbsp black or white sesame seeds (optional)

salt and ground black pepper

mango chutney, to serve

SAUSAGE-LESS ROLLS

Nobody wants to miss out on sausage rolls! Luckily, you don't have to. These have a punchy mushroom filling, full of umami flavour. You can make individual rolls, as here, or why not try making a giant one that you can cut into slices and serve as a filling main dish. A giant roll will take about 10–15 minutes more to cook.

MAKES 8 * PREP 30 MINS + COOLING * COOK 40–50 MINS

- 1 tbsp vegetable oil
- 1 red onion, peeled and finely chopped
- 300g/11oz mushrooms, finely chopped
- 50g/2oz/¼ cup chopped walnuts
- 10 sun-dried tomatoes, chopped
- 50g/2oz/¼ cup chopped black olives
- 2 tbsp soy sauce
- 50g/2oz/½ cup fresh breadcrumbs
- 275g/10oz vegan puff pastry, thawed if frozen
- plain/all-purpose flour, for dusting
- vegan margarine, melted, for brushing
- salt and ground black pepper

1. Heat the oil in a large, deep frying pan, add the onion, season with salt and pepper and cook for 10 minutes, until the onion is soft. Add the mushrooms and cook for 2 minutes more, then stir in the walnuts, sun-dried tomatoes, olives and soy sauce and cook for 5 minutes, stirring occasionally. Remove from the heat and stir in the breadcrumbs.

2. Spoon the mixture into the food processor and using the pulse button, whiz until the mixture is combined but still retains some texture. Alternatively, chop it all together on a board using a large knife. Leave to cool.

3. Preheat the oven to 200°C/400°F/Gas 6. Roll the pastry out on a lightly floured surface to about 15 × 25cm/6 × 10in and cut it in half lengthways. Spoon half the mixture down one side of one strip of pastry, wet the edges with a little water and fold over the other side of pastry. Press together the edges with the back of a fork to seal. Repeat with the other strip and remaining filling mixture.

4. Brush the top of the pastry parcels with some melted margarine, to glaze, then slice each parcel into 4 sausage rolls, so you have 8 in total. Slash the top of each one, to let steam out, and transfer them to 2 baking sheets, spacing them well apart.

5. Put in the oven and bake for 20–30 minutes, until puffed and golden. Remove from the oven and serve hot or at room temperature.

CHILLI 'NON' CARNE

Packed with flavour and fun to eat, chilli is a popular choice in many households. This is a really 'meaty' version made with soya mince and kidney beans, which are high in protein and keep you full for ages. Set out the accompaniments in separate bowls and let people put together their preferred combinations at the table.

SERVES 4 ✱ PREP 15 MINS ✱ COOK 55 MINS

1. Heat the oil in a large frying pan, add the onion, season with salt and pepper and cook on a low heat for about 10 minutes or until softened.

2. Stir in the garlic, fresh chilli and cayenne pepper if using, and cook for 1 minute more. Stir in the peppers and cook for few minutes to soften.

3. Add the soya mince, kidney beans and sweetcorn and stir until well combined. Pour in the stock, bring to the boil, then reduce to a simmer and cook for about 40 minutes, topping up with more hot water as required. The soya mince should absorb all the water but you don't want it to be dry.

4. Serve with boiled rice, tortilla chips, avocado, sour cream, lime wedges and fresh coriander.

COOK'S NOTE

✱ Adjust the spiciness to suit, and remember that you can always add heat by drizzling over a little chilli oil once it has been served if you want your portion to be a bit spicier, but you can't take heat away.

✱ The same applies for fresh coriander/cilantro. Some people don't like it, so serving it separately gives everyone the option.

Vegan Hack

To make vegan sour cream, simply mix 250ml/8fl oz/1 cup vegan single/light cream with the juice of 1 lemon, then leave it for 15 minutes to thicken and sour.

1 tbsp vegetable oil

1 onion, peeled and finely chopped

2 garlic cloves, peeled and finely chopped

½–1 fresh red chilli, seeded and finely chopped

a pinch of cayenne pepper (optional – use sparingly, it is hot!)

1 red bell pepper, seeded and chopped

1 yellow bell pepper, seeded and chopped

450g/1lb/2 cups soya mince

400g/14oz can of red kidney beans, drained (optional)

340g/11½oz can of sweetcorn, drained

900ml/1½ pints/3¾ cups hot vegetable stock

salt and ground black pepper

TO SERVE

boiled brown or white rice (see box on page 143)

tortilla chips

2 avocados, halved, stoned and sliced (toss in lemon juice to prevent them discolouring)

250ml/8fl oz/1 cup vegan sour cream (bought, or see hack)

lime slices

a handful of fresh coriander/ cilantro leaves

COTTAGE PIE

The whole family will enjoy this meat-free version of a cottage pie – filled with high-protein beans in a delicious gravy sauce, topped with creamy mash. This is ideal make-ahead food, and also freezes really well so you could double up and have a pie ready for another day.

SERVES 4 * PREP 30 MINS * COOK 1 HR

1 tbsp vegetable oil

1 onion, peeled and finely chopped

2 garlic cloves, peeled and finely chopped

3 carrots, peeled and diced

1 tbsp tomato paste

1 tbsp brown sauce or ½ tbsp yeast extract

2 × 400g/14oz cans of aduki beans, drained

900ml/1½ pints/3¾ cups hot vegetable stock

salt and ground black pepper

FOR THE MASH

900g/2lb potatoes, peeled and quartered

50g/2oz/¼ cup vegan margarine, plus extra for topping

about 3 tbsp vegan milk

salt and ground black pepper

1. Heat the oil in a large, deep frying pan, add the onion, season with salt and pepper and cook for 10 minutes, until the onion is soft. Mix in the garlic and carrots and cook for about 4 minutes, then add the tomato paste, brown sauce and aduki beans and stir so everything gets combined.

2. Pour in the stock, bring it to the boil, then reduce it to a simmer and leave it to cook gently for 30 minutes. If it starts to dry out at all, top up with a little hot water.

3. Meanwhile, make the mash. Boil the potatoes in a large pan of salted water, with the lid ajar, for about 20 minutes, until tender when you poke them with a knife. Drain well, then tip them back into the pan. Put the lid on and sit the pan (off heat) to steam-dry for 5 minutes.

4. Remove the lid and let the steam clear, then add the vegan margarine and mash well to remove any lumps. Pour in the milk and add salt and pepper, then mash until really creamy. Taste and adjust the seasoning as needed.

5. Preheat the oven to 200°C/400°F/Gas 6. Spoon the aduki bean mixture into an ovenproof dish, then cover with the mashed potato, run the back of a fork over the mash to make a pattern, and dot over a little margarine.

6. Cook for about 20 minutes or until turning golden and bubbling. Remove from the oven and serve – on its own or with cooked peas, broccoli or sweetcorn or even some baked beans on the side.

VEGETABLE MOUSSAKA WITH TOFU TOPPING

This vegan adaptation of the famous Greek dish has all the savoury succulence of the traditional version. A flavoursome almond and tofu topping is used instead of the usual egg-enriched dairy-heavy béchamel. Aubergines in a mushroomy sauce create a substantial and tasty filling.

SERVES 8 * PREP 30 MINS * COOK 50–60 MINS

1. Preheat the grill or broiler to high. Place the aubergine slices in one layer on the rack. Lightly brush with 2 tbsp of the oil and grill for 2–3 minutes on each side until golden. Alternatively, sear them in batches in a very hot heavy frying pan or skillet. Put to one side while you make the sauce.

2. Heat the remaining 2 tbsp oil in a large pan and fry the onions, garlic and carrots for 5–7 minutes. Add the courgettes, mushrooms, canned tomatoes, vinegar, yeast extract and nutmeg to the pan and season with salt and pepper. Bring to the boil, then simmer for 20 minutes.

3. Meanwhile, make the topping. Toast the ground almonds in a heavy frying pan, without any oil, for 1–2 minutes, until golden, tossing occasionally.

4. Put the toasted almonds in a food processor or blender and add the tofu, ketchup, soy sauce, lemon juice and mustard powder. Process the mixture until smooth and well combined. Taste and adjust the seasoning as required.

5. Preheat the oven to 180°C/350°F/Gas 4. Spread half the sauce in a 35 × 23cm/14 × 9in ovenproof dish. Add a layer of aubergine slices and spread over the remaining sauce. Finish with a layer of aubergine slices.

6. Spoon the topping over the aubergine slices, ensuring it is spread evenly. Bake for about 20–25 minutes, until the topping is set and has turned golden brown. Garnish with a sprinkling of paprika and some fresh basil leaves. Serve immediately.

600g/1lb 8oz aubergines/eggplants, cut into 2.5cm/1in slices

4 tbsp vegetable oil

2 large onions, coarsely chopped

2 garlic cloves, peeled and crushed

2 large carrots, peeled and finely chopped

4 courgettes/zucchini, sliced

200g/7oz mushrooms, sliced

2 × 400g/14oz cans of chopped tomatoes

2 tbsp balsamic vinegar

4 tsp yeast extract

1 tsp ground nutmeg

salt and ground black pepper

FOR THE TOPPING

75g/3oz/¾ cup ground almonds

350g/12oz silken tofu

2 tbsp tomato ketchup

1 tbsp soy sauce

1 tbsp lemon juice

½ tsp English/hot mustard powder

salt and ground black pepper

ground paprika and fresh basil leaves, to garnish

JACKFRUIT HOTPOT WITH DUMPLINGS

This is a good way to gets lots of healthy veg into one dish. The dumplings are easy to make and turn this into a really filling dish, but you could make it without them if you prefer, and simply serve the hotpot with some crusty bread.

SERVES 4–6 * PREP 30 MINS * COOK 1 HR 30 MINS

1 tbsp vegetable oil

1 onion, peeled and finely chopped

3 celery sticks, finely chopped

3 carrots, peeled and cut into chunky pieces

2 sweet potatoes, peeled and cut into chunky pieces

1 tbsp tomato paste

a handful of fresh thyme stalks, leaves only, chopped

1 tbsp tamari

1 tbsp peanut butter

900ml/1½ pints/3¾ cups hot vegetable stock

200g/7oz/1 cup vacuum-packed jackfruit pieces

salt and ground black pepper

FOR THE DUMPLINGS

250g/9oz/2¼ cups self-raising/self-rising flour

2–3 tbsp finely chopped flat leaf parsley

140g/4½oz/½ cup vegan hard margarine, chilled and cut into cubes

150ml/¼ pint/⅔ cup water

1. Preheat the oven to 180°C/350°F/Gas 4. Heat the oil in a large ovenproof casserole dish, add the onion, season with salt and pepper and cook for 10 minutes, until the onion is soft. Add the celery and carrots and cook for 4–5 minutes, then stir in the sweet potatoes and turn so everything is combined.

2. Add the tomato paste, thyme, tamari and peanut butter and stir again. Pour in the stock and bring it to the boil, put the lid on and put it in the oven for 1 hour. Keep an eye on it to check that it isn't drying out at all – add a splash of boiling water if necessary. Add the jackfruit for the last 15 minutes, stirring it in so it is covered with the stock.

3. Meanwhile, prepare the dumplings. Put the flour, herbs, salt and pepper in a large bowl, and using your fingertips, rub the margarine into the flour until it resembles breadcrumbs. Slowly stir in the water until it comes together as a dough.

4. Pull out walnut-sized balls. You should be able to make about 12 dumplings, depending on how big they are.

5. Remove the pan from the oven and arrange the dumplings on top, pushing them slightly under the stock. Put the lid on and return the pan to the oven for another 15–20 minutes, until the dumplings are puffed up and golden. Remove from the oven and serve immediately.

VARIATION

If you want to make cheesy dumplings, stir 115g/4oz/1 cup grated vegan Cheddar-style cheese into the dumpling mix before adding the water.

SPICY TOFU STIR-UP

This Indian-style dish is made with odds and ends that are already in the kitchen. It has a wonderful confetti of colours and a fabulous mingling of hot and spicy flavours.

SERVES 4 * PREP 20 MINS * COOK 25 MINS

1. Heat 2 tbsp of the oil in a non-stick pan until it reaches smoking point, then reduce the heat slightly and add the tofu (you may need to add in batches). Stir-fry for about 3-4 minutes, until it turns golden, remove and put to one side.
2. Heat another 1 tbsp oil, then add the carrots, cook for about 3-4 minutes until golden, then remove with a slotted spoon and drain on kitchen paper. Brown the cauliflower in the oil remaining in the pan for about 3 minutes, then remove and drain the fried florets on kitchen paper.
3. Add the remaining 1 tbsp of oil to the pan and heat until the oil is about to smoke. Switch off the heat source and add all the ingredients for the five-spice mix. Let it crackle and pop for about 30 seconds.
4. Add the bay leaves, coriander, cumin, turmeric and chilli powder. Place the pan over a low heat and fry the spices for about 1 minute.
5. Add the golden tofu and carrots, and pour in 300ml/½ pint/¼ cup lukewarm water. Bring it to the boil, reduce the heat to low and cover the pan.
6. Cook for 5–6 minutes, then add the fried cauliflower, the shredded cabbage, peas and salt.
7. Cover and simmer for 4–5 minutes, then add the chillies, chopped tomatoes and coriander. Cook, uncovered, for 2–3 minutes. Remove from the heat and serve, with boiled rice and flatbreads if you like.

COOK'S NOTE

You can either buy pre-mixed five-spice mix or make your own, as here. The curry is quite hot so reduce the fresh green chillies if you prefer.

4 tbsp vegetable oil

175g/6oz firm tofu, drained and cut into 2.5cm/1in cubes

115g/4oz carrots, peeled and cut into 2.5cm/1in cubes

150g/5oz cauliflower, cut into 2.5cm/1in florets

2 bay leaves

1 tsp ground coriander

1 tsp ground cumin

½ tsp ground turmeric

½ tsp chilli powder

½ a small cabbage (about 200g/7oz), finely shredded

115g/4oz/1 cup garden peas, fresh or frozen (boiled until tender, if fresh)

1 tsp salt, or to taste

4–5 fresh green chillies, seeded (use fewer if you prefer less heat)

2 ripe tomatoes, cut into chunks

a bunch of fresh coriander/cilantro leaves, chopped

flatbreads and boiled rice, to serve (see box on page 143)

FOR THE FIVE-SPICE MIX

½ tsp black or brown mustard seeds

½ tsp cumin seeds

½ tsp fennel seeds

½ tsp nigella seeds

6 fenugreek seeds

KORMA CURRY

This mild curry is creamy and fragrant, making it suitable for all the family. It is packed with colourful veg and protein-rich chickpeas and can be adapted to use up whatever veg you have to hand. Serve it with rice, poppadoms, chutney and yogurt for an Indian-inspired feast.

SERVES 4 * PREP 20 MINS * COOK 1 HR

1 tbsp vegetable oil

1 onion, peeled and finely chopped

5cm/2in piece of fresh root ginger, peeled and finely chopped

½–1 fresh red chilli, seeded and finely chopped (optional)

3 carrots, peeled and sliced

1 butternut squash, halved, seeded, peeled and cut into bite-size pieces

2 tbsp garam masala

1 tbsp tomato paste

50g/2oz/½ cup ground almonds

400g/14oz can of chopped tomatoes

400g/14oz can of chickpeas/garbanzos, drained (reserve the aquafaba liquid for another recipe)

about 500ml/17fl oz/2 cups hot water

200g/7oz/1¾ cups frozen peas, defrosted

250ml/8fl oz/1 cup vegan single/light cream

a handful of fresh coriander/cilantro leaves, chopped (optional)

salt and ground black pepper

TO SERVE

poppadoms

vegan Greek-style plain yogurt

mango chutney

boiled brown or white rice (see box on page 143)

1. Heat the oil in a large, heavy pan, add the onion, season with salt and pepper and cook for 10 minutes, until the onion is soft. Stir in the ginger and chilli if using, cook for a minute more, then add the carrots and butternut squash and cook, stirring occasionally, for 3–4 minutes.

2. Stir in the garam masala, tomato paste and ground almonds, then add the chopped tomatoes, chickpeas and hot water and bring to the boil. Reduce to a simmer and cook for about 40 minutes, topping up with hot water if it starts to dry out at all.

3. Stir in the peas and heat for a few minutes, then stir in the vegan cream and fresh coriander, if using. Taste and season some more if it needs it.

4. Serve up the curry with rice, poppadoms, yogurt and chutney on the side.

Vegan Hack

Always save the liquid from a can of chickpeas/garbanzos as the aquafaba may come in handy for another recipe. Pour it into a sealed container and keep it in the fridge for a few days or freeze it for up to 1 month. Defrost before using.

MUSHROOM STROGANOFF

A stroganoff is a Russian dish that is usually made with steak and mushrooms. This vegan mushroom version is full of flavour and creaminess, and is much healthier and lower in saturated fat than the original.

SERVES 4 * PREP 15 MINS * COOK 20 MINS

1 Heat the oil in a large frying pan, add the onion, season with salt and pepper, and cook for 10 minutes until the onion is soft. Stir in the garlic and cook for a further 1 minute.

2 Add the mushrooms and stir around the pan, then cook for 3–4 minutes. Stir in the mustard and paprika, add the stock and let it bubble for a few minutes. Stir in the cream and simmer it for a few minutes more.

3 Taste and season some more if it needs it, then transfer to serving dishes and sprinkle over a little paprika and parsley to garnish. Serve with rice.

1 tbsp vegetable oil

1 onion, peeled and finely chopped

2 garlic cloves, peeled and finely chopped

500g/1¼lb chestnut and white button mushrooms, sliced

2 tsp Dijon mustard

2 tsp paprika, plus extra for serving

250ml/8fl oz/1 cup hot vegetable stock

250ml/8fl oz/1 cup vegan single/light cream

salt and ground black pepper

a large handful of fresh parsley, finely chopped, to garnish

boiled rice, to serve (see box)

How to Cook Rice

For 4 people, put 200g/7oz/1 cup rice in a sieve or strainer and rinse it well under cold running water. Drain it, then put in a pan and pour in enough water to come about 5cm/2in above the rice. Season with a pinch of salt, put a lid on and cook gently over a medium heat for about 15 minutes, until tender. Remove the pan from the heat and leave it to stand with its lid on for a few minutes to continue steaming. The water should have been absorbed but you can drain off any excess. Serve.

TOMATO NO-MEAT-BALL BAKE

These meatless balls are a cinch to make and have a really substantial texture and savoury flavour, meaning they'll be a hit with everyone. Here, they are baked in a rich, garlicky tomato sauce and served with spaghetti. This is a good dish to make ahead and reheat, as the flavours only get better!

SERVES 4 * PREP 30 MINS + COOLING + 30 MINS CHILLING * COOK 1 HR

1. To make the no-meat balls, first cook the rice. Put it in a small pan and pour over enough water so it comes about 5cm/2in above the rice. Add a pinch of salt, cover with the lid ajar and cook for about 20 minutes or according to the packet instructions, until tender. Top up with a little more hot water if it starts to dry out too much. The rice should absorb all the water. Put it to one side and leave it to cool.

2. Put the beans, onion, garlic, walnuts, oats, soy sauce and miso in a food processor, season with salt and pepper and add the cold rice. Whiz until everything is combined. It's up to you how smooth you want the meatless balls to be. If you want a bit of texture, don't over-whiz the mixture. If you don't have a food processor, put everything on a large board and chop and scrape it all together until it is fairly smooth.

3. Wet your hands and roll the mixture into balls. Place them on a baking sheet and put them in the fridge for 30 minutes to chill and firm up.

4. Meanwhile, make the sauce. Heat the oil in a large, deep frying pan, add the chopped onion, season with salt and pepper and cook for 10 minutes, until the onion is soft. Stir in the garlic and cook for a further minute. Tip in the tomatoes and stock and bring to the boil, then reduce to a simmer and cook for 20 minutes, topping up with hot water if it starts to dry out at all.

5. To cook the meatballs, heat a little of the oil in a large frying pan or skillet and add a few meatballs (fry them in batches). Cook for 3–4 minutes on each side until golden and cooked. Tip on to a piece of kitchen paper to drain while you fry the remaining balls.

6. Add the cooked balls to the tomato sauce and let them simmer gently for about 15 minutes. Garnish with parsley and serve on their own or with some cooked pasta.

cooked spaghetti or other pasta, to serve

chopped fresh parsley, to garnish

FOR THE NO-MEAT-BALLS

50g/2oz/¼ cup brown rice, rinsed

400g/14oz can of black beans, drained and rinsed

1 red onion, peeled and finely chopped

2 garlic cloves, peeled and finely chopped

50g/2oz/¼ cup chopped walnuts

50g/2oz/½ cup rolled oats

1 tbsp soy sauce

1 tbsp brown rice miso

a little vegetable oil, for frying

salt and ground black pepper

FOR THE TOMATO SAUCE

1 tbsp olive oil

1 onion, peeled and finely chopped

2 garlic cloves, peeled and finely chopped

2 × 400g/14oz cans of chopped tomatoes

1.2 litres/2 pints/5 cups vegetable stock

salt and ground black pepper

SWEDISH-STYLE MEATLESS BALLS WITH CHIPS & JELLY SAUCE

Here's another way to serve up the meatless balls from page 144. Instead of the Italian-style tomato sauce, they are cooked in a thick gravy and served Scandi-style with some chips on the side.

SERVES 4 ✱ PREP 30 MINS + COOLING + 30 MINS CHILLING ✱ COOK 30 MINS

meatless balls (see page 144)

a little vegetable oil, for frying

cranberry jelly, to serve

FOR THE FRIES

6 medium potatoes, peeled and sliced into fine chips

1–2 tbsp vegetable oil

a pinch of salt

FOR THE GRAVY

900ml/1½ pints/3¾ cups hot vegetable stock

about 2 tsp cornflour/cornstarch

about 2 tsp cold water

1 tbsp cranberry jelly

1 Preheat the oven to 200°C/400°F/Gas 6. Put the potato chips in a large roasting pan, add the oil and salt and turn everything together using your hands. Put in the oven and cook for 20–30 minutes, until crisp and golden. Keep an eye on them as they can burn easily.

2 Meanwhile, fry the meatless balls. Heat a little oil in a large frying pan or skillet and add a few meatballs (fry them in batches). Cook for 3–4 minutes on each side until golden and cooked. Tip on to a piece of kitchen paper to drain while you fry the remaining balls.

3 To make the gravy, put the vegetable stock in a pan and heat it up. Blend the cornflour and water to a smooth paste, add it to the stock and stir continually, until it starts to thicken and is smooth. If it starts to get lumpy at all, switch to a balloon whisk and beat until smooth. Stir in the cranberry jelly and heat until it has melted. If the gravy is too thick, add a little more hot water; if it is a little too thin, mix an additional 1 tsp cornflour blended with 1 tsp water and stir this in to thicken it.

4 Add the cooked meatless balls to the gravy and simmer gently for about 10 minutes. Serve with the fries and cranberry jelly on the side.

Look Out!

Check the label of the cranberry jelly to ensure it does not contain gelatine.

TOMATO SOUP WITH CROÛTONS

This is especially good in the summer, when tomatoes are ripe and full of flavour, but you can also make it using canned chopped tomatoes during the rest of the year. Served with chunky croûtons, it makes a filling lunch or supper.

SERVES 4 * PREP 20 MINS * COOK 30 MINS

1 Heat the oil in a large frying pan, add the onion, season with salt and pepper, and cook for 10 minutes until the onion is soft. Stir in the garlic and cook for a minute more, then add the celery and carrot and cook, stirring occasionally, for 4–5 minutes, until softened.

2 Add the tomatoes, tomato paste and balsamic vinegar, stir around the pan and let them cook for a few minutes so the flavours mingle and intensify. Pour in the stock, bring to the boil, then reduce to a simmer and cook for about 20 minutes, until the veg are really soft. Turn off the heat.

3 Meanwhile, preheat the oven to 200°C/400°F/Gas 6. Toss the bread cubes with olive oil and grated cheese and arrange the pieces on a baking sheet. Put in the oven for 10–15 minutes, until crisp and golden. Remove and put to one side.

4 Carefully ladle the tomato soup from the pan into a blender. Blitz until smooth. You will have to do this in batches. Return the soup to the pan to reheat it if necessary. Alternatively, use a hand-held blender and process it in the pan.

5 Ladle the hot soup into bowls and top with the crisp croûtons. Serve immediately.

VARIATION

For a cream of tomato soup, simply stir in 200ml/7fl oz/1 cup vegan single/light cream towards the end of the cooking time.

1 tbsp vegetable oil

1 red onion, peeled and finely chopped

2 garlic cloves, peeled and finely chopped

2 celery sticks, trimmed and finely chopped

1 carrot, trimmed and finely chopped

6 tomatoes, roughly chopped

1 tsp tomato paste

a splash of balsamic vinegar

1.2 litres/2 pints/5 cups hot vegetable stock

salt and ground black pepper

FOR THE CROÛTONS

4 slices of crusty bread, cut into chunky squares

a drizzle of olive oil

115g/4oz/1 cup vegan Cheddar-style cheese, grated

SWEETCORN & NOODLE SOUP

This is the easiest soup you will ever make. It's so satisfying, and is just as good in hot or cold weather. Be prepared to slurp while eating – it's compulsory!

SERVES 4 * PREP 10 MINS * COOK 20 MINS

275g/10oz rice noodles

340g/11½oz can of sweetcorn

1 tbsp vegetable oil

a bunch of spring onions/scallions, trimmed and finely chopped

a pinch of chilli flakes (optional)

1–2 tbsp soy sauce

1.2 litres/2 pints/5 cups hot vegetable stock

salt and ground black pepper

1. Soak the rice noodles in hot water as per the packet instructions, then drain well and set aside.
2. Whiz half the can of corn, with all of its juice, in a food processor until it is smooth and creamy.
3. Heat the oil in a large deep pan, add the spring onion and season with salt and pepper. Cook for 3–4 minutes, until soft, then stir in the chilli flakes if using, along with the creamed sweetcorn and the remaining whole sweetcorn kernels.
4. Add the soy sauce, stir and add the stock. Bring to the boil, then reduce to a simmer and cook gently for 15 minutes.
5. Taste and add a splash more soy sauce if it needs it, then stir in the soaked and drained rice noodles, heat through and ladle into bowls.

VARIATION

You could stir through some cooked and sliced vegan 'chicken' pieces to make an almost-chicken and noodle soup.

250ml 1C

SNACKS **NIBBLES** & **LIGHT** BITES

ORANGE & CARROT
BERRY NICE
GORGEOUS GREEN

SMOOTHIES 3 WAYS

You can really pack some goodness into a smoothie – they're an appealing and convenient way to boost your fruit and veg intake. Unlike juices, they retain the natural fibre of the ingredients, which is better for your insides and also helps to keep you feeling full for longer.

ORANGE & CARROT

This vivid smoothie is a perfect balance of natural sweetness. You'll need to chop the carrots finely, or even grate them, so they blend to a smooth texture, and you'll need a powerful blender to handle the ice cubes. If you're not sure, grate the carrots and use iced water rather than ice cubes.

SERVES 2

PREP 5 MINS

4 oranges, peeled and roughly chopped (saving and using as much juice as possible)

275g/10oz carrots, peeled and roughly chopped

200g/7oz ice cubes or 250ml/8fl oz/1 cup ice-cold water

1 Put everything into the blender and whiz until smooth and combined.
2 Drink immediately or put in the fridge until you're ready to serve, giving it a mix before drinking.

BERRY NICE

This smoothie is satisfying and delicious, almost like thawed frozen yogurt – sure to appeal to those who like ice cream! Depending on how tart the berries are you may need to adjust the sweetness, but start with just a little maple syrup and taste it before you add too much – it may not need it.

SERVES 2

PREP 5 MINS

300ml/½ pint/1¼ cups vegan milk

115g/4oz/½ cup vegan plain yogurt

1 banana, peeled and roughly chopped

250g/9oz frozen berries

2 tsp maple syrup

1 Put everything into the blender and whiz until smooth and combined.
2 Drink immediately or put in the fridge until you're ready to serve, giving it a mix before drinking.

GORGEOUS GREEN

Spinach has quite a strong flavour, but it's sweetened and balanced in this thick smoothie by some apple and banana. Coconut water is especially good for hydration since it contains natural electrolytes (which are often added to sports recovery drinks), making this a healthy smoothie to enjoy after a workout. You could just use water if you prefer.

SERVES 2

PREP 5 MINS

50g/2oz spinach leaves

1 sweet eating apple, peeled and cored

1 small banana, peeled and roughly chopped

250ml/8fl oz/1 cup coconut water or water

1 Put everything into the blender and whiz until smooth and combined.
2 Drink immediately or put in the fridge until you're ready to serve, giving it a mix before drinking.

SAVOURY SCRAMBLE BAGELS

Silken tofu is a fabulous high-protein alternative to use for scrambled eggs, since it has a similar texture and carries flavour really well. Here, turmeric, mustard and nutritional yeast flakes are used, and the scramble is served with tasty slices of tempeh in soy sauce on a toasted bagel. Now that's a snack to get excited about!

SERVES 4 * PREP 10 MINS * COOK 10 MINS

150g/5oz tempeh, sliced thinly
1 tbsp soy sauce
350g/12oz silken tofu
2 tbsp vegetable oil
2 tsp ground turmeric
1 tsp Dijon mustard
1 tbsp nutritional yeast flakes
4 bagels, halved and toasted
vegan margarine, for spreading (optional)
salt and ground black pepper
a little chopped fresh parsley, to garnish

1. In a shallow bowl, toss the tempeh slices in the soy sauce and set aside.
2. Put the silken tofu in another bowl and mash with a fork, leaving a bit of texture.
3. Heat half the oil in a frying pan, add the mashed tofu and stir. Season with salt and pepper, turmeric, mustard and nutritional yeast, then stir well and cook gently for 5–6 minutes until heated through.
4. Meanwhile, heat the remaining oil in another frying pan. Add the soy-marinated tempeh and cook for a couple of minutes on each side or as per packet instructions, until golden and crispy.
5. Spread the warm toasted bagels with margarine if using, then divide the scramble between them and top with slices of tempeh. Garnish with chopped parsley and serve.

VARIATION

You could stir through peeled and chopped fresh tomatoes and/or chopped fresh coriander/cilantro leaves, and even add a dash of mild curry powder for a spicy alternative.

FRENCH TOAST WITH RASPBERRIES & MAPLE SYRUP

Crisp on the outside, soft in the middle, and flavoured with warming spices, French toast is an irresistible choice for a quick snack, breakfast or brunch. Serve it with some fresh fruit and a drizzle of maple syrup for a decadent treat, or even with some vegan 'bacon' if you want to go Canadian-style.

SERVES 2 * **PREP 10 MINS** * **COOK 10 MINS**

120ml/4fl oz/½ pint vegan milk

a pinch of ground nutmeg

a pinch of ground cinnamon

1 tbsp sugar

50g/2oz/¼ cup vegan margarine

4 slices of sourdough bread or bread of your choice

TO SERVE

a handful of raspberries or blueberries

vegan crème fraîche, vegan Greek-style plain yogurt or whipped vegan cream

maple syrup

an extra sprinkle of ground nutmeg and cinnamon

1. In a bowl, beat together the milk, nutmeg, cinnamon and sugar and put to one side.
2. Melt a little of the margarine in a frying pan (you will need to cook 2 slices at a time). Brush each slice of bread liberally with the milk mixture to cover each side, then put the bread in the frying pan.
3. Cook each side for about 2–3 minutes, until golden. Repeat with the other slices of bread.
4. Transfer the French toast to serving plates and top with raspberries or blueberries, a spoonful of crème fraîche, yogurt or whipped cream, a drizzle of maple syrup and a dusting of ground nutmeg and cinnamon.

PANCAKES

Pancakes are delicious at any time of the day, and make a great brunch or sweet snack. This recipe is for the thin crêpe-style pancakes rather than fluffier American-style ones. Serve them filled with whatever you fancy, and then roll up for easy eating.

MAKES 6–8 * **PREP 5 MINS** * **COOK 15–20 MINS**

1. In a large bowl, whisk together the flour, baking powder and sugar, then make a dip in the middle. Pour in the aquafaba, i.e. the juice from the canned chickpeas, and the milk, and whisk until the batter is smooth and lump-free.
2. Heat a drizzle of the oil in a non-stick frying pan. When it's hot, add a ladleful of batter and tip the pan so it covers the surface in an even layer. Cook for about 1 minute, loosen the edges with a spatula and leave it to cook a little longer, until it loosens from the pan in the middle when you give it a shake.
3. Flip over the pancake with the spatula – or toss it in the air if you are feeling brave – and cook the other side for about 1 minute, until golden. Transfer to a plate.
4. Repeat, heating a little oil as you go, until all the batter has gone. It's best to serve the pancakes as soon as they come out of the pan, so everyone will have to wait patiently while you cook them to order. Serve with your favourite toppings.

300g/11oz/2⅔ cups self-raising/self-rising flour

1 tsp baking powder

1 tbsp caster/superfine sugar

liquid from 400g/14oz can of chickpeas/garbanzos

400ml/14fl oz/1⅔ cups vegan milk

1–2 tbsp vegetable oil, for cooking

TO SERVE

sliced banana and maple syrup

sliced strawberries, blueberries and maple syrup

vegan chocolate spread

RED PESTO BREAD
GARLIC BREAD

HOT BAGUETTES

Baked baguettes are delicious in their own right, but here they are taken to the next level with the addition of some seriously garlicky butter in one and tasty tomato pesto in the other.

GARLIC BREAD

It is so easy to make this irresistible snack using a vegan butter and plenty of garlic. As for the corn on the cob on page 86, it's worth trying to find hard-block vegan butter for this particular recipe, though you can use regular vegan margarine if that's what you have.

SERVES 2–4

PREP 10 MINS

COOK 15–20 MINS

1 baguette or French stick

115g/4oz/½ cup vegan butter

4 garlic cloves, peeled and finely chopped or grated

a handful of flat leaf parsley leaves, finely chopped

1 Preheat the oven to 200°C/400°F/Gas 6. Make deep cuts along the top of the bread, being careful not to go the whole way through.
2 In a bowl, beat together the butter, garlic and parsley, then spoon the mixture into each slash.
3 Wrap the bread in foil, twisting the ends securely, and bake it in the oven for 15–20 minutes, until golden and all the butter has melted into the bread. Unwrap, tear or slice, and serve.

RED PESTO BREAD

A jar of vegan sun-dried tomato pesto is instant and easy, but you can also use your own home-made red or orange pesto (see pages 43 and 44). For a cheesy twist, grate some vegan Cheddar-style cheese or slice some vegan mozzarella-style cheese and stuff into the slashes after you've spread the pesto.

SERVES 2–4

PREP 10 MINS

COOK 15–20 MINS

1 baguette or French stick

about 4 tbsp vegan sun-dried tomato pesto

1 Preheat the oven to 200°C/400°F/Gas 6. Make deep cuts along the top of the bread, being careful not to go the whole way through.
2 Spoon in the pesto, wrap the bread in foil, twisting the ends securely, and bake it in the oven for 15–20 minutes, until golden. Unwrap from the foil, and tear off slices to eat.

MINI POTATO SKINS WITH TOMATO & SWEETCORN SALSA

These mini skins are perfect for snacking, packed lunch or for party food, since they can be eaten hot or cold. Using small potatoes cuts down on the cooking time, as well as making them a better size for sharing.

SERVES 4–6 * PREP 30 MINS + COOLING TIME * COOK 35–40 MINS

1. Preheat the oven to 200°C/400°F/Gas 6. Prick the potatoes and toss them in 1 tbsp olive oil, put on a baking sheet, and bake in the hot oven for about 20 minutes or until just soft.

2. If you prefer, you can cook the new potatoes in a microwave. Prick them with a fork and put them in a microwave-proof bowl, in a single layer if possible. Microwave on High for 4 minutes, then give them a stir and cook for a further 4 minutes. Be careful when you take them out of the microwave as they will be really hot.

3. When the potatoes are cool enough to handle, halve them and carefully scoop out the insides. Put the soft cooked potato insides into a bowl, season with salt and pepper, and stir in the cheese and spring onions. Put to one side.

4. Sit the skins on a baking sheet outer side up, brush them with another tbsp of oil, then bake in the oven for 10–15 minutes or until golden and crispy.

5. Remove the baking sheet from the oven, turn the potato skins up the other way and fill each one with a spoonful of the potato mixture. Return them to the oven for a further 15 minutes, until golden.

6. Meanwhile, make the salsa. Mix together the tomato, sweetcorn and oil and season with salt and pepper.

7. Serve the potatoes with the salsa and some vegan mayonnaise on the side.

500g/1¼lb new potatoes

1–2 tbsp olive oil

115g/4oz/1 cup vegan Cheddar-style cheese, grated

4 spring onions/scallions, trimmed and finely chopped

salt and ground black pepper

vegan mayonnaise, to serve

FOR THE SALSA

4 tomatoes, finely chopped

200g/7oz can of sweetcorn, drained

1 tbsp extra virgin olive oil

salt and ground black pepper

CAULI MUNCHIES

These crispy cauliflower bites make a great alternative to carb- and fat-loaded chips, and taste just as good hot or cold. Here, they are served with a simple yogurt dip, but you could also serve them with hummus, a quick tomato relish (see page 170) or just some tomato ketchup.

SERVES 4 * PREP 5 MINS * COOK 5 MINS

2 tbsp olive oil

1 tbsp za'atar spice mix

2 garlic cloves, peeled and thinly sliced

1 head of cauliflower, cut into florets

1 tsp mild paprika

a pinch of coarse salt

TO SERVE

200g/7oz/1 cup vegan Greek-style plain yogurt

3 tbsp fresh chopped mint

1. Heat the oil in a large non-stick frying pan, add the za'atar spice mix and garlic and fry over a low heat for 1 minute to release the flavour of the spice mix.
2. Add the cauliflower and increase the heat to medium, then stir-fry for 3–4 minutes, until the cauliflower is just beginning to brown around the edges and is hot but still crisp.
3. Sprinkle with the paprika and a little salt, and serve the munchies on their own or with the yogurt flavoured with the chopped mint.

COOK'S NOTE

Za'atar spice mix is made up of sesame seeds, dried thyme, oregano, sumac and cumin seeds and is available in larger supermarkets or ethnic grocers. It is popular all over the Middle East and is often sprinkled over flatbreads before baking.

FRIED VEGAN MOZZARELLA STICKS

These cheesy sticks coated in crisp breadcrumbs are delicious with a tomato-based salsa or a sweet chilli dipping sauce. You can prepare ahead for a snack or party food, then bake to heat up just before serving.

MAKES 20 * PREP 20 MINS + 20 MINS FREEZING * COOK 5 MINS

1. Cut the cheese in half lengthways and then into 1cm/½in strips. Keep these in the fridge, covered, while preparing the other ingredients.
2. Put the chickpea flour in a bowl with a pinch of salt, the onion powder and the herbs if using. Blend to a paste with a little of the milk, then stir in the rest. Put the plain flour in a second bowl and the breadcrumbs in a third bowl.
3. Using a pair of forks, dip a cheese stick into the batter. Shake off the excess, then dip into the flour and turn to coat. Shake off the excess, dip into the batter again, then into the breadcrumbs, turning to coat all over. Place on a baking tray lined with baking parchment.
4. Repeat with the remaining cheese sticks, then freeze for 20 minutes to ensure they are really firm.
5. Heat about 2cm/¾in of oil in a large frying pan until hot (check by dropping in a small cube of stale bread; it should brown within 30 seconds). Taking care – ask an adult to help if you aren't one – lower in the cheese sticks a few at a time; don't overcrowd the pan or the temperature of the oil will drop. Cook for about 30 seconds or until the breadcrumbs are dark golden and crisp, carefully turning them over halfway.
6. Using a slotted spoon, lift out the mozzarella sticks on to a plate lined with kitchen paper and keep warm while cooking the rest in the same way. Serve at once with a dipping sauce, tomato relish or ketchup.

250g/9oz vegan mozzarella-style cheese

2 tbsp chickpea/gram flour

a pinch of salt

½ tsp onion powder (optional)

½ tsp dried mixed herbs (optional)

120ml/4fl oz/½ cup vegan milk

50g/2oz/½ cup plain/all-purpose flour

90g/3½oz/scant 1 cup fresh white breadcrumbs

sunflower oil, for shallow frying

tomato salsa (see page 123), quick tomato relish (see below), chilli dipping sauce or ketchup, to serve

Quick Tomato Relish

For a quick tomato relish, mix together 6 tbsp tomato ketchup, 2 tsp malt vinegar and 8 red or yellow cherry tomatoes, finely chopped. Stir in 1 tbsp chopped fresh herbs such as parsley or basil.

HUMMUS
RED PEPPER HUMMUS
GUACAMOLE

DIPS 3 WAYS

Dips served with chopped veg, breadsticks or tortilla chips hit the spot when you get an attack of the munchies. Here are three all-time classics, which also happen to work well in sandwiches or as accompaniments to other dishes.

HUMMUS

Making your own hummus is incredibly easy – just whiz everything up in a food processor and you're done! Made with high-protein chickpeas, it is not only tasty and healthy, but it also helps you stay full for longer.

SERVES 4–6

PREP 5 MINS

400g/14oz can of chickpeas/garbanzos, drained

2 garlic cloves, peeled and crushed

3 tbsp tahini

about 200ml/7fl oz/1 cup extra virgin olive oil

juice of ½–1 lemon

salt and ground black pepper

1 Put the chickpeas in a food processor along with the garlic and tahini, and whiz until combined and finely chopped. Slowly trickle in the olive oil until it is the right consistency.
2 Now add a little lemon juice and salt and pepper, taste, then add more salt and lemon juice if it needs it. If it is too thick, add a splash of just-boiled water.
3 Transfer the hummus to a bowl and serve with dippers.

RED PEPPER HUMMUS

The addition of roasted red pepper from a jar makes this hummus so much sweeter – totally addictive. Pep things up if you like it hot, with a pinch of chilli flakes.

SERVES 4

PREP 5 MINS

1 portion of home-made hummus (left)

4 roasted red bell peppers from a jar

a pinch of chilli flakes (optional)

1 Add the roasted red peppers and the chilli flakes, if using, to the hummus mixture in the food processor and whiz until combined.
2 Transfer the hummus to a bowl and serve with your choice of dippers.

Get Dipping!

Try carrot sticks, bell pepper strips, cucumber sticks, mangetout, radishes and cherry tomatoes.

GUACAMOLE

There are countless recipes for guacamole – some containing chopped tomato, onion and fresh coriander/cilantro, others consisting purely of avocado, salt and lime juice. This version includes some chopped tomato for sweetness and texture.

SERVES 4

PREP 20 MINS

1 tomato

3 ripe avocados, halved, stoned and flesh removed

2 garlic cloves, peeled and grated

juice of 1 lime

salt and ground black pepper, to taste

1 Skin the tomato (slice a cross on the bottom, put in a bowl with boiling water to cover for 30 seconds, then plunge the tomato into cold water and remove the skin). Chop the flesh.
2 Put the avocado in a bowl with the garlic, lime juice, salt and pepper. Lightly mash it with a fork – you still want some texture – then stir in the tomato.
3 Transfer the guacamole to a bowl and serve with dippers.

CHILLI CASHEWS
SALTED ALMONDS
MAPLE-FLAVOURED PECANS

NUTS 3 WAYS

Nuts, for those who can eat them, are the ultimate nibble when you're feeling peckish. Here are three different ways to enjoy them: sweet, salty and spicy. Just do remember to check before you offer them to guests, in case of nut allergies, and don't take them anywhere near school.

CHILLI CASHEWS

Cashew nuts work really well with spices. These ones pack a bit of a punch, but you can just use less cayenne pepper and leave out the chilli flakes if you can't take the heat.

SERVES 4–6

PREP 10 MINS

COOK 10 MINS

225g/8oz/2 cups cashew nuts

2 tsp paprika

½ tsp cayenne pepper

pinch chilli flakes

1 Preheat the oven to 200°C/400°F/Gas 6. Spread out the nuts in a single layer on a baking sheet, then toss with the paprika, cayenne pepper and chilli flakes.

2 Put in the oven and roast for about 10 minutes, until golden, keeping a close eye on them to check they don't burn. Leave to cool, then transfer to serving bowls.

SALTED ALMONDS

These nuts are so addictive – be prepared for the fact that they will disappear in a flash. It's best to use almonds with their skins on, which have a better flavour when roasted, and by happy chance also contain more fibre. You could also use blanched whole almonds if that's what you have to hand.

SERVES 4–6

PREP 5 MINS

COOK 5 MINS

½ tsp vegetable oil

225g/8oz/2 cups unblanched almonds

a generous pinch of sea salt

1 Heat the oil in a large frying pan, add the nuts and salt and cook for 3–4 minutes, moving them around continually so they don't burn and to coat the almonds in the salty oil.

2 Remove from the heat, allow to cool and transfer to serving dishes.

MAPLE-FLAVOURED PECANS

Pecans are naturally quite sweet and have a real affinity with maple syrup – just think of pecan pie! These nibbles are perfect when you fancy something sweet but still healthy.

SERVES 4–6

PREP 5 MINS

COOK 10 MINS

225g/8oz/2 cups pecan nuts

4 tbsp maple syrup

1 Preheat the oven to 200°C/400°F/Gas 6. Spread out the nuts in a single layer on a baking sheet, drizzle over maple syrup, then stir the two together really well.

2 Put in the oven and roast for about 10 minutes, until golden and sticky, keeping a close eye on them to check they don't burn. Leave to cool, then transfer to serving bowls.

QUICK-ROAST CHICKPEAS

Chickpeas are great in more things than hummus. Try them as a super-speedy spiced alternative to crisps. Low in fat, they make a good protein-rich snack, and as chickpeas contain complex carbs they take longer for the body to break down, giving a slow-release energy boost.

SERVES 4 * PREP 5 MINS * COOK 10 MINS

1. Rinse the chickpeas in a colander with cold water, drain, then dry with kitchen paper.
2. Warm the oil in a large frying pan, then add the cumin, fennel and sesame seeds and cook over a medium heat for 1 minute to release the flavour. Take the pan off the heat and stir in the paprika.
3. Tip the chickpeas into the frying pan, sprinkle with the ground linseeds and stir well to coat in the spice mix. Cook over a medium-high heat, stirring, for about 5 minutes, until the spice forms a dry crust.
4. Drizzle with the maple syrup, sprinkle with a little salt and fry briefly until the syrup has caramelized. Leave to cool – eat while just warm, or cooled completely.

VARIATION

If you like chilli or foods with a bit of heat then add ¼ tsp hot smoked paprika instead of the mild or sweet version. It has the same kind of heat as chilli powder but with the addition of a lovely smoky barbecue flavour.

400g/14oz can of chickpeas/garbanzos, drained

4 tsp vegetable oil

1 tsp cumin seeds, roughly crushed

½ tsp fennel seeds, roughly crushed

1 tbsp sesame seeds

1 tsp mild smoked paprika

1 tbsp ground linseeds

2 tsp maple syrup

a pinch of salt

VEG CRISPS

We all know it's easy to grab a packet of bought crisps, but if you have a bit of time it's fun to make your own in all sorts of different colours and flavours. Even better, nobody can tell you off for munching them as they are made from healthy vegetables.

SERVES 2 * PREP 10 MINS * COOK 20–30 MINS

1. Preheat the oven to 140°C/275°F/Gas 1. Toss the sliced parsnips with 1 tbsp of the oil then lay them, well spaced out, on a large baking sheet.
2. Toss the beetroot with the remaining olive oil, then lay them out on a separate baking sheet, well spaced out.
3. Put them all in the oven and bake for 20–30 minutes or until crisp and golden, but be careful they don't burn.
4. Remove from the oven and allow to cool. Transfer to serving bowls and sprinkle with a pinch of sea salt.

2–3 large parsnips, peeled and finely sliced

2 tbsp olive oil

2–4 balls of raw beetroot, peeled and finely sliced

a pinch of sea salt

POP
CORN

POPCORN 3 WAYS

If you love popcorn, you will be thrilled when you discover how easy it is to make your own. Just make sure you do not lift that pan lid until all the corn has finished popping or it will go everywhere!

SALTED POPCORN

Sometimes the simplest things are the best, and that's certainly the case when it comes to popcorn. All it needs is a little salt to enhance its natural flavour. Irresistible.

SERVES 2–4

PREP 1 MIN

COOK 5 MINS

4 tbsp vegetable oil

1 tsp salt

50g/2oz/⅓ cup popcorn kernels

1 Heat the oil and salt in a large pan with a tight-fitting lid. Once it is hot, drop in 3 corn kernels and put the lid on. When they pop, remove the pan from the heat, wait for 30 seconds, then tip in all the popcorn kernels, stir well, put the lid back on and put it back on the heat.

2 Now wait until all the popcorn has all popped, shaking the pot occasionally, and holding the lid on tight. Remove the pan from the heat.

3 Transfer the popcorn to serving bowls or one large bowl and dig in!

SWEET POPCORN

This has more calories than the salted popcorn, but if you fancy something sweet, this will really hit the spot.

SERVES 2–4

PREP 5 MINS

COOK 10 MINS

4 tbsp vegetable oil

50g/2oz/⅓ cup popcorn kernels

225g/8oz/1 cup vegan margarine

4 tbsp maple syrup or agave nectar

1 Heat the oil in a large pan with a tight-fitting lid. Once it is hot, drop in 3 corn kernels and put the lid on. When they pop, remove the pan from the heat, wait for 30 seconds, then tip in all the popcorn kernels, stir well, put the lid back on and put it back on the heat.

2 Now wait until all the popcorn has popped, shaking the pot occasionally, and holding the lid on tight. Remove the pan from the heat.

3 Melt the margarine and maple syrup or agave nectar together in a small pan, bring to the boil, then simmer for 5 minutes until it darkens and thickens slightly. Pour the caramel into the popped pcorn and stir until it is all coated.

4 Leave it to cool slightly, then transfer the sweet popcorn to serving bowls.

SALTY & SWEET!

If you want a mix of sweet and salty popcorn, make the salty one first then combine it with the sweet one, mixing well.

COOK'S NOTE

You can also make popcorn in the microwave, which means less washing up if you make it in the bowl you serve it in. Simply put the corn kernels, oil and salt in a large microwave-safe bowl, stir to completely coat the kernels in oil, then cover with a vented lid. Cook on High for 3–4 minutes, or until the rate of popping slows to one pop every 2 seconds or so. The timing will vary from microwave to microwave so play it by ear and listen. When the popping stops, the scoffing starts!

CAKES COOKIES & SWEET TREATS

CELEBRATION CHOCOLATE CAKE

It's good to have a fabulous foolproof vegan chocolate cake in your repertoire – bake it for celebrations, birthdays or just because! This is smothered in a chocolate buttercream and grated chocolate, but you could dust the cake in icing sugar or cocoa powder for a less fancy affair.

SERVES 8–12 * PREP 30 MINS + COOLING * COOK 40–45 MINS

175g/6oz/scant 1 cup caster/superfine sugar

250g/9oz/2¼ cups self-raising/self-rising flour

50g/2oz/½ cup unsweetened cocoa powder

1 tsp bicarbonate of soda/baking soda

1½ tsp baking powder

150ml/¼ pint/⅔ cup sunflower oil, plus extra for greasing

2 tsp vanilla extract

1½ tbsp apple cider vinegar

300ml/½ pint/1¼ cups vegan milk

2 tbsp vegan plain yogurt

FOR THE BUTTERCREAM AND DECORATION

100g/3¾oz vegan dark/bittersweet chocolate (70% cocoa solids), plus a little extra for grating on top

300g/11oz/1 cup plus 6 tbsp, vegan butter

250g/9oz/2¼ cups icing/confectioner's sugar

vegan white chocolate, for grating on top (optional)

1. Preheat the oven to 180°C/350°F/Gas 4. Grease two 20cm/8in round cake pans and line the bases with greaseproof paper.

2. Sift all the dry ingredients together into a large bowl and make a dip in the middle. In a jug or pitcher, mix together the oil, vanilla extract, apple cider vinegar, milk and yogurt, then pour into the dry ingredients and beat to combine

3. Divide the mixture evenly between the cake pans, level the tops with a spatula, and put in the oven to bake for 35–40 minutes or until risen and a skewer comes out clean when poked into the middle.

4. Remove the cakes from the oven and leave to cool for 10 minutes in the pan, then loosen around the edges with a knife, release them from the pans and sit the sponges on a wire rack to cool completely.

5. Meanwhile, make the buttercream. Melt the chocolate in a bowl set over a pan containing a little simmering water – make sure the bottom of the bowl doesn't touch the water. Stir the chocolate occasionally. Put to one side.

6. Beat the butter until smooth in a food processor, or in a bowl with a hand-held beater or just a wooden spoon and some muscle power. Sift in the icing sugar and beat until combined and smooth. If it needs more icing sugar, sift in a little more, then add the chocolate and beat again until smooth.

7. Cover one half of the cake with some of the buttercream and sandwich the cakes together, then spread the remaining buttercream over the top and sides of the cake. It doesn't have to be perfectly smooth. Grate over the dark and white chocolate, if using, and leave it to set. Slice to serve. Store in an airtight container for up to 3 days.

VANILLA SPONGE CAKE WITH JAM & CREAM

Traditionally, a Victoria sandwich cake is sandwiched together with raspberry jam and dusted with icing sugar. Here, a vanilla sponge cake is sandwiched with strawberry jam and vegan cream. It is light, airy and moist. It is best eaten on the day it is made.

SERVES 8–12 * PREP 20 MINS + COOLING * COOK 30–35 MINS

225g/8oz/1 cup vegan soft margarine, plus extra for greasing
300g/11oz/1½ cups caster/superfine sugar
200g/7oz/1 cup vegan plain yogurt
100ml/3½fl oz/½ cup sunflower oil
200ml/7fl oz/1 cup vegan milk
2 tsp vanilla extract
400g/14oz/3½ cups self-raising/self-rising flour
2 tsp baking powder

FOR THE FILLING AND TOPPING

a few squirts of ready-whipped vegan cream from a canister
about 3 tbsp strawberry or raspberry jam
about 3 tbsp icing/confectioner's sugar
a handful of fresh strawberries, hulled and some halved

1. Preheat the oven to 180°C/350°F/Gas 4. Grease two 20cm/8in round cake pans and line the bases with greaseproof paper.

2. Put the soft margarine and sugar in the bowl of a food mixer, and using the beater attachment, beat for about 10 minutes, until creamy and fluffy. Alternatively, use a bowl and a hand-held beater, or a wooden spoon and some muscle power.

3. In a jug or pitcher, mix the yogurt, oil, milk and vanilla, then add to the butter and sugar mixture along with a large spoonful of the flour, and continue beating until combined. Sift in half of the remaining flour and beat to combine, then sift in the rest of the flour and the baking powder and gently fold them in using a spoon. The mixture will have lots of air in it now that will help it to rise.

4. Divide the mixture evenly between the pans, level the tops with a spatula, and put in the oven to bake for 30–35 minutes or until golden and risen and a skewer comes out clean.

5. Remove the cakes from the oven and leave to cool for 10 minutes in the tin, then loosen around the edges with a knife, release the sponges from the pans and set on a wire rack to cool.

6. Spread one sponge with jam and squirt over a layer of cream, then top with the other sponge. Using a sieve, dust over icing sugar and top with strawberries. Eat the same day, but if you leave off the cream and strawberries it will keep in an airtight container for 2 days.

Vegan Hack

If you don't want to use squirty cream from a canister, you can make some whipped coconut cream instead. Simply put a can of full-fat coconut milk in the fridge overnight to chill. When you want to use it, open the can and scoop the very thick cream that has risen to the surface into a bowl. Using a balloon whisk or hand-held beater, whisk this until it is light and has increased in volume. Delicious!

CUPCAKES 3 WAYS

Cupcakes are so cute and are great for sharing with friends. They are also really quick to make, so you can whip up a batch in no time at all. Here are three favourites – vanilla, lemon and chocolate – for you to try. Decorate or leave them simply iced, it's entirely up to you.

BASIC CUPCAKE MIXTURE

This basic method makes enough for 9 good-sized cupcakes, or a larger number of small fairy cakes if you prefer. Fill the cases to about two-thirds of the way up the sides so that they look the same and don't overflow. Flavour, bake and decorate as described in the individual recipes that follow.

MAKES 9

PREP 10 MINS

225g/8oz/2 cups self-raising/self-rising flour

1 tsp bicarbonate of soda/baking soda

1 tsp baking powder

a pinch of salt

175g/6oz/1½ cups caster/superfine sugar

200ml/7fl oz/1 cup vegan milk

1½ tsp apple cider vinegar

2 tbsp vegan plain yogurt

1 Sift together all the dry ingredients into a large bowl and make a dip in the middle. In a jug or pitcher, mix the milk, cider vinegar and yogurt.

2 Pour the wet mixture into the flour mix and beat well to combine.

SIMPLE VANILLA CUPCAKES

Sometimes you just want a really simply little cake to hit that sweet spot. These are especially good for bake sales or parties as they are easy to serve up in their individual cases and the scope for decorating is (almost) limitless.

MAKES 9

PREP 20 MINS + COOLING

COOK 20–25 MINS

1 quantity of cupcake mixture (see left)

2 tsp vanilla extract

For the decoration:

225g/8oz/2 cups icing/confectioner's sugar

about 2–3 tbsp warm water

sprinkles or other decorations

1 Line a 9-hole cupcake tin/pan with paper cases. Preheat the oven to 180°C/350°F/Gas 4.

2 Make the cupcake batter, adding the vanilla extract to the wet ingredients in the jug or pitcher and blending before adding to the dry ingredients.

3 Divide the mixture evenly between the paper cases.

4 Put in the oven to bake for 20–25 minutes or until golden and risen and a skewer comes out clean when poked into the middle. Remove from the oven, put the cakes on a wire rack and leave to cool.

5 While the cakes are cooling, make the icing. Sift the icing sugar into a bowl then slowly mix in the warm water, a little at a time, until you get a stiff icing.

6 Spoon the icing over the top of the cooled cakes and decorate as liked. Leave to set. Store in an airtight container for up to 3 days.

continued page 196 >

LEMON BUTTERFLY CUPCAKES

These light lemon sponges are topped with lemon buttercream and have their tops cut off and turned into wings for extra appeal. This isn't at all difficult to do but looks sweet. Just make sure the sponge is completely cold before you try to cut it.

MAKES 9

PREP 20 MINS + COOLING

COOK 20–25 MINS

1 quantity of cupcake mixture (page 193)

juice and zest of 1 lemon

For the decoration:

175g/6oz/¾ cup vegan butter

225g/8oz/2 cups icing/ confectioner's sugar, sifted, plus extra for dusting

juice of ½–1 lemon

1 Line a 9-hole cupcake tin/pan with paper cases. Preheat the oven to 180°C/350°F/Gas 4.
2 Make the cupcake batter, adding the lemon juice and zest to the wet ingredients in the jug or pitcher and blending before adding to the dry ingredients.
3 Divide the mixture evenly between the paper cases.
4 Put in the oven to bake for 20–25 minutes or until golden and risen and a skewer comes out clean when poked into the middle. Remove from the oven, put the cakes on a wire rack and leave to cool.
5 While the cakes are cooling, make the lemon buttercream. Beat the butter with the icing sugar until smooth, then add the lemon juice. If it is too wet, add a little more sifted icing sugar and if it gets too stiff, add a few drops of warm water.
6 Slice a circle out of the top of each cake, then slice the circle in half to make the butterfly wings. Spoon or pipe the icing into the hole in each cake, then sit in the wings. Dust with icing sugar to serve. Store in an airtight container for up to 3 days.

CHOCOLATE MAPLE CUPCAKES

Maple syrup really lifts the chocolate buttercream for these tasty little cakes. When baking any chocolate cake, it's really important to keep an eye on them because it's harder to see from their colour when they are done, and also because cocoa powder can make them a bit dry if they are over-baked. Start testing after 20 minutes and whip them out as soon as the skewer comes out clean.

MAKES 9

PREP 20 MINS + COOLING

COOK 20–25 MIN

1 quantity of cupcake mixture (page 193)

2 tbsp unsweetened cocoa powder

2 tsp vanilla extract

For the decoration:

175g/6oz/¾ cup vegan butter

225g/8oz/2 cups icing/ confectioner's sugar, sifted

2 tsp unsweetened cocoa powder

2 tsp maple syrup

vegan dark/bittersweet chocolate (70% cocoa solids) curls or grated chocolate, to decorate

1 Line a 9-hole cupcake tin/pan with paper cases. Preheat the oven to 180°C/350°F/Gas 4.
2 Make the cupcake batter, sifting the cocoa powder with the flour and other dry ingredients, and adding the vanilla extract to the wet ingredients in the jug or pitcher and blending before adding to the dry ingredients.
3 Divide the mixture evenly between the paper cases.
4 Put in the oven to bake for 20–25 minutes or until risen and a skewer comes out clean when poked into the middle. Remove from the oven, put the cakes on a wire rack and leave to cool.
5 While the cakes are cooling, make the chocolate and maple buttercream. Beat the butter and icing sugar together. Mix the cocoa powder with 2 tsp warm water and add it and the maple syrup to the butter mixture, and beat until smooth.
6 Pipe or spoon the icing on to the cooled chocolate cakes. Top with chocolate curls or grated chocolate, if using. Store in an airtight container for up to 3 days.

COOK'S NOTE

Chocolate curls are really easy to make but look super-impressive. Simply hold a bar of cold chocolate over a plate and run a Y-shaped vegetable peeler down the side to create curls. That's it!

LEMON BUTTERFLY CUPCAKES
CHOCOLATE MAPLE CUPCAKES
SIMPLE VANILLA CUPCAKES

LEMON DRIZZLE CAKE

The perfect combination of sweet and tart. Sugary lemon syrup infuses the cake and creates a crunchy topping. This is a really easy bake, is super-moist and tangy, and guaranteed to be a crowd-pleaser.

SERVES 8 * PREP 20 MINS * COOK 30–35 MINS

1 Preheat the oven to 190°C/375°F/Gas 5. Line a 450g/1lb loaf tin/pan with a paper liner, or grease and line it with greaseproof paper.

2 Sift the flour, sugar, baking powder and bicarbonate of soda into a large bowl and stir in the lemon zest. Make a dip in the middle.

3 In a jug, blend the oil, yogurt and lemon juice until combined, then pour into the flour mixture and beat until smooth. Scrape the cake batter into the prepared loaf tin.

4 Put it in the oven and bake for about 30–35 minutes, until golden and a skewer comes out clean when it's poked in the middle. Remove from the oven and put to one side in the tin while you make the topping.

5 Make the syrup. Combine the lemon juice and sugar in a bowl. Using a skewer, poke holes in the top of the cake and pour over the lemon and sugar mix.

6 Leave the cake to cool, then remove it from the tin and put it on a wire rack. Slice to serve. Store in an airtight container for up to 3 days.

275g/10oz/2½ cups self-raising/self-rising flour, sifted

200g/7oz/1 cup caster/superfine sugar

1½ tsp baking powder

1 tsp bicarbonate of soda/baking soda

juice and zest of 1 lemon

100ml/3½fl oz/½ cup sunflower oil, plus extra for greasing

200g/7oz/1 cup vegan plain yogurt

FOR THE SYRUP

75g/3oz/scant ½ cup caster/superfine sugar

juice of 1 lemon

PUMPKIN GINGERBREAD TRAYBAKE

Traybakes are great when you need to feed a crowd, or even just when you want lots of cake at home! This is a dense gingerbread sponge, made lovely and moist by adding pumpkin purée, and decorated with cute but simple icing sugar gingerbread men.

MAKES 24 * PREP 10 MINS + 15 MINS SOAKING + COOLING * COOK 25–35 MINS

1. Mix the ground flaxseed and water in a small bowl and set aside for 15 minutes to form a gel. Preheat the oven to 180°C/350°F/Gas 4. Grease and line a 35 × 25cm/14 × 10in deep baking tin/pan.
2. Sift the flour into a large mixing bowl with the baking powder, bicarbonate of soda, spices, vanilla powder (if using) and salt.
3. In a pan, heat the margarine, treacle, syrups and dark brown sugar until the sugar has melted.
4. Remove from the heat and leave to cool slightly. Stir in the milk and vanilla extract (if using). Pour the syrup mixture into the flour mixture and whisk in. Whisk in the pumpkin purée, yogurt and flaxseed gel, and then pour and scrape the batter into the prepared tin.
5. Bake for 25–35 minutes, until the cake is firm and a knife comes out clean with no batter on it when inserted into the middle of the cake. Remove from the oven and leave the cake in the tin on a wire rack to cool.
6. To decorate, cut the cake into 24 squares and dust with icing sugar. For the cute gingerbread decoration, cut out a small figure shape from a piece of paper as a template and place on a square of cake. Dust over icing sugar, then carefully remove the paper template. Press small white sugar pearls into the cakes as eyes and buttons. Repeat with the other squares. Store in an airtight container for up to 5 days.

COOK'S NOTE

You can make pumpkin purée but it is simpler to use canned.

- 2 tbsp ground flaxseeds
- 6 tbsp water
- 550g/1¼lb/scant 5 cups plain/all-purpose flour
- 1 tsp baking powder
- 1 tsp bicarbonate of soda/baking soda
- 1 tsp ground cinnamon
- 1 tsp ground ginger
- 1 tsp ground mixed spice/pumpkin pie spice
- 1 tsp vanilla powder or vanilla extract
- a pinch of salt
- 250g/9oz/1 cup plus 2 tbsp vegan margarine, plus extra for greasing
- 175g/6oz/½ cup treacle/molasses
- 175g/6oz/½ cup golden/light corn syrup
- 2 tbsp ginger syrup
- 150g/5oz/¾ cup soft dark brown sugar
- 175ml/6fl oz/¾ cup vegan milk
- 400g/14oz pumpkin purée
- 250g/9oz/1¼ cups vegan Greek-style plain yogurt
- icing/confectioner's sugar, for dusting
- small white sugar pearls, for decorating

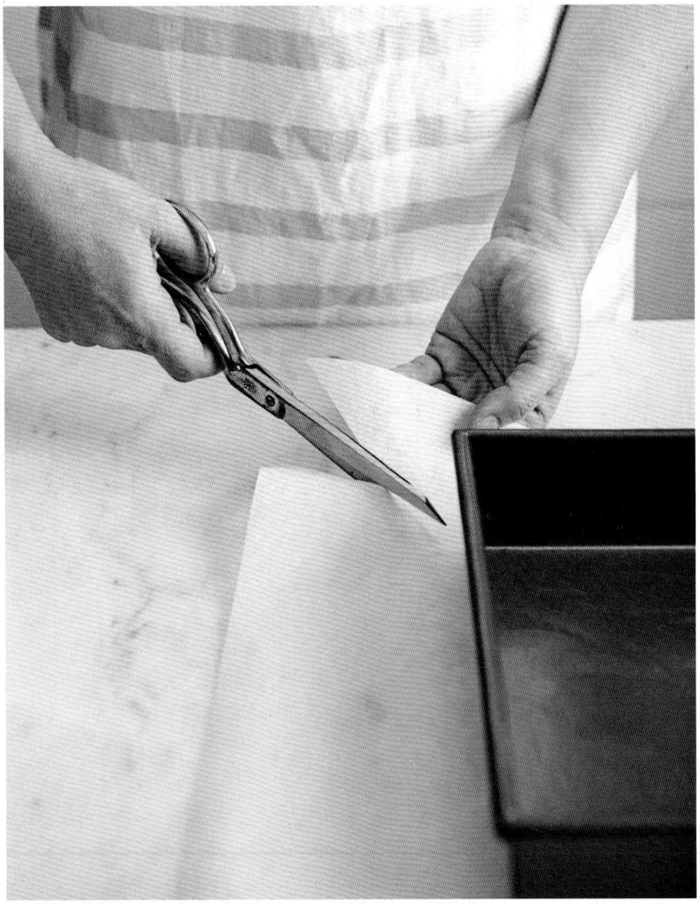

CHOCOLATE BROWNIES

These bake a little differently from a version containing eggs – but are deliciously squidgy and intensely chocolatey. They also only get better with time, so if you don't manage to eat them straight away, put the tray in the fridge overnight for an even fudgier texture.

MAKES 12 * PREP 20 MINS * COOK 25–30 MINS

1. Preheat the oven to 190°C/375°F/Gas 5. Grease and line a baking tin/pan that measures about 20 × 30cm/8 × 12in.
2. Position a heatproof bowl over a pan of just-simmering water, making sure the bottom of the bowl doesn't touch the water. Put the chocolate and margarine in the bowl and let it melt, stirring occasionally, until smooth.
3. Sift together the flour and cocoa powder into a large bowl, then stir in the chickpea liquid (aquafaba), both sugars and the vanilla extract. Stir in the melted chocolate.
4. Pour and scrape the brownie batter into the tin and bake for 25–30 minutes, until just set. A skewer inserted into the middle should have some damp mixture on it.
5. Leave to cool in the tin, then drizzle over the melted white chocolate, if using, and slice into squares to serve. Store in an airtight container for up to 3 days.

COOK'S NOTE

Don't over-bake your brownies or else they will become cakey rather than fudgey.

200g/7oz vegan dark/bittersweet chocolate (70% cocoa solids)

175g/6oz/¾ cup vegan margarine, plus extra for greasing

115g/4oz/1 cup plain/all-purpose flour

50g/2oz/½ cup unsweetened cocoa powder

liquid (aquafaba) from a 400g/14oz can of chickpeas/garbanzos

90g/3½oz/½ cup caster/superfine sugar

75g/3oz/⅓ cup dark muscovado sugar

1 tsp vanilla extract

100g/3¾oz vegan white chocolate, melted, for the topping (optional)

HOME FROM SCHOOL FLAPJACK

This is one of the easiest sweet traybakes you can make – simply melt, stir and bake. This recipe uses agave syrup instead of golden syrup, though you could use golden syrup instead if that's what you have. Agave syrup is really sweet so you don't need much.

MAKES 12 * **PREP 15 MINS** * **COOK 35–45 MINS**

1. Preheat the oven to 160°c/325°F/Gas 3. Grease and line a 20cm/8in square cake tin/pan.
2. Put the margarine, sugar and agave syrup in a large pan and let it melt, stirring occasionally, then stir in the porridge oats until everything is really well combined.
3. Spoon the mixture into the tin and flatten it with the back of a spoon. Put it in the oven and bake for 30–40 minutes or until golden.
4. Remove from the oven and let it cool in the tin for about 15 minutes, then slice into squares and leave it to cool completely before removing it from the tin. Store in an airtight container for up to a week.

VARIATIONS

You could stir in your favourite dried fruit to this mix – sultanas, apricots, cranberries or cherries – or stir in a handful of nuts if you prefer (just don't take it to school if you add any nuts).

225g/8oz/1 cup vegan margarine, plus extra for greasing

225g/8oz/1 cup demerara sugar

2 tbsp agave syrup

275g/10oz/3 cups rolled oats

CHOCOLATE SHORTBREAD BARS

Shortbread is such an easy bake and only needs three ingredients: margarine, sugar and flour. You can eat it as it is or topped with chocolate as here, or even add a layer of caramel (see box) for a really indulgent Millionaire's Shortbread!

MAKES 16 * PREP 15–30 MINS + COOLING * COOK 30–40 MINS

115g/4oz/½ cup vegan margarine, plus extra for greasing

50g/2oz/¼ cup caster/superfine sugar

175g/6oz/1½ cups plain/all-purpose flour

100g/3¾oz vegan dark/bittersweet chocolate (70% cocoa solids)

1. Preheat the oven to 180°C/350°F/Gas 4. Grease and line a 18cm/7in square tin/pan.
2. Put the margarine and sugar in a food processor and whiz until combined and smooth, then add the flour and pulse until it comes together as a dough. Alternatively, beat together the butter and sugar in a bowl with a hand-held mixer or a wooden spoon, then stir in the flour.
3. Transfer the dough to the tin, patting it down gently so it is flat, and prick it all over with a fork. Put it in the oven to bake for about 30 minutes, until just pale golden and firm to the touch. Remove from the oven and leave to cool.
4. To make the chocolate topping, sit a heatproof bowl over a pan of just-simmering water, making sure the base of the bowl doesn't touch the water. Put the chocolate in the bowl and stir occasionally until it melts. Pour the chocolate over the shortbread and smooth to cover. Leave it to cool.
5. Slice into bars and serve. Store in an airtight container for up to 3 days.

COOK'S NOTE

Don't over-bake shortbread – you don't want it to brown or it will become hard and will shatter when you try to cut it.

Millionaire's Topping

To make a caramel layer, pour a 320g/11½oz can of sweetened condensed milk, 100g/3¾oz/8 tbsp vegan margarine and 100g/3¾oz/½ cup dark brown sugar in a heavy pan and place over a medium heat. Stir until dissolved, then turn the heat up and boil the mixture for 5–6 minutes, until it thickens and turns golden. Stir constantly and stay with it, taking great care as caramel is hot and burns easily (ask an adult to help if necessary).

Pour the caramel over the baked shortbread, after step 3. Leave it to cool and set completely before covering with the melted chocolate.

CHOC CHIP COOKIES

Cookies are a fun and easy bake to make, and even more so to eat. These ones are crisp on the outside and chewy in the middle – just how they should be. You could switch in other flavours of vegan chocolate, or use a combination, or maybe add some chopped nuts.

MAKES 20 * **PREP 20 MINS + 20 MINS** * **COOK 12–15 MINS**

1. In a big bowl or in the bowl of a food mixer, beat together the margarine and sugars until creamy, then beat in the flour, bicarbonate of soda and salt.

2. Stir in the chocolate pieces, then put the bowl in the fridge for 20 minutes for the mixture to chill and firm up (you can leave it longer or overnight if you wish).

3. Preheat the oven to 160°C/325°F/Gas 3. Lightly grease a couple of baking sheets.

4. When you're ready to bake, scoop up walnut-sized pieces of the mixture and roll into 20 balls. Place them on the baking sheets, leaving some room between them, then flatten each one with your hands.

5. Put in the oven and bake for 12–15 minutes. They may still look a bit squidgy but they will harden as they cool. Leave them on the baking sheets for 5 minutes, then transfer them to wire racks to cool completely. Store in an airtight container for up to 3 days.

COOK'S NOTE

You could make double the quantity of dough, so you can bake half now and wrap and freeze the other half for up to 1 month. Defrost before using.

150g/5oz/¾ cup vegan margarine, plus extra for greasing

100g/3¾oz/½ cup caster/superfine sugar

100g/3¾oz/½ cup dark brown sugar

225g/8oz/2 cups plain/all-purpose flour

1 tsp bicarbonate of soda/baking soda

a pinch of salt

200g/7oz vegan dark/bittersweet chocolate (70% cocoa solids), bashed with a rolling pin and chopped into small pieces

PEANUT BUTTER COOKIES

These nutty cookies are made from ingredients you'll probably have in your cupboard and fridge already – so there's no excuse not to get your bake on!

MAKES 14–16 * PREP 20 MINS + 20 MINS CHILLING * COOK 12–15 MINS

1. In a big bowl or in the bowl of a food mixer, beat all of the ingredients until they come together as a dough.
2. Scoop the mixture out from the bowl, transfer it to greaseproof/waxed paper and roll it in the paper to form a large sausage shape. Put this in the fridge for 20 minutes to chill and firm up.
3. Preheat the oven to 180°C/350°F/Gas 4 and grease a couple of baking sheets.
4. Slice the dough into discs and place these on the prepared baking sheets, leaving plenty of room between them as they will spread, then gently press each one with your hand to flatten.
5. Put in the oven and bake for 12–15 minutes, until pale golden, then remove from the oven and leave them to harden for at least 5 minutes. Transfer the cookies to wire racks to cool completely. Store in an airtight container for up to 3 days.

100g/3¾oz/¾ cup plain/all-purpose flour

100g/3¾oz/½ cup soft light brown sugar

75g/3oz/6 tbsp vegan margarine, plus extra for greasing

2 tbsp sugar-free crunchy peanut butter

1 tsp bicarbonate of soda/baking soda

a pinch of salt

NO-BAKE CHEESECAKE

There are two main types of cheesecake: ones that are baked, and ones that are set using gelatine (for non-vegans) or agar agar, as here. There are infinite variations for flavours and toppings. This recipe keeps things simple, and consists of a biscuit base topped with a creamy lemony mixture. Decorate with fresh strawberries, and if you like, pour on a strawberry coulis.

SERVES 8 * PREP 20 MINS + CHILLING * COOK 5 MINS

100g/3¾oz/8 tbsp vegan margarine, plus extra for greasing

300g/11oz vegan digestive biscuits/graham crackers

400g/14oz vegan cream cheese

250ml/8fl oz/1 cup vegan single/light cream

115g/4oz/1 cup icing/confectioner's sugar

zest and juice of 2 lemons

3 tsp agar agar mixed with 1 tbsp water

FOR THE TOPPING

a handful of fresh strawberries, some halved

strawberry coulis (optional, see box)

icing/confectioner's sugar, for dusting (optional)

1. Grease and line a 20cm/8in springform round cake tin/pan. Melt the margarine in a large pan.
2. Meanwhile, put the digestives in a strong plastic bag and bash to crumbs with a rolling pin, or else blitz them in a food processor. Stir the crumbs into the margarine until combined, then tip the mixture into the base of the tin and press it down in an even layer. Put in the fridge to chill and firm up.
3. In a big bowl or food mixer, beat the cream cheese, cream, icing sugar and lemon zest and juice, until combined.
4. Heat the agar agar in a small pan with the water until it boils, adding a splash more water if it is too thick to pour, then pour it into the cream cheese mix and beat until combined.
5. Pour the cream cheese mixture over the biscuit base and put it in the fridge to chill and set.
6. Release the cheesecake from the tin, drizzle over the coulis if you have made some, top with strawberries and sift over icing sugar, if liked. Store in the fridge for up to 2 days.

Strawberry Coulis

Put about 8 strawberries, roughly chopped, in a small pan with a splash of water and heat gently. Bring to the boil for 1 minute, then pour through a strainer set over a bowl so you collect the juice. Return the juice to the pan and bubble again until it starts to thicken a little. Remove from the heat and leave to cool, ready to pour over your cheesecake.

MINI MERINGUES

Some clever alchemy happens when you use the juice from a can of chickpeas as it whisks up light and foamy, similar to egg white. The texture of vegan meringue is different and can be quite delicate, which is why we've made several smaller ones, but you can make a larger one if you prefer. Fragility aside, they taste great – these are finished off with a squirt of cream and topped with kiwis, but you can choose your favourite fruit.

SERVES 6–8 * PREP 10 MINS * COOK 1 HOUR 15 MINS

1. Preheat the oven to 140°C/275°F/Gas 1. Line a baking sheet with baking parchment and draw 6–8 circles on it, each about 7.5cm/3in round.

2. Put the chickpea liquid (the aquafaba) in the bowl of a food mixer, or use a hand-held beater, and whisk for 5–8 minutes, until foamy and soft peaks form. Slowly tip in the sugar and keep whisking until the peaks become quite firm.

3. Spoon the meringue mixture into the prepared circles on the baking parchment, then put it in the oven to bake for 1 hr 15 mins, until crisp.

4. Leave to cool completely, then very carefully remove the meringues from the baking parchment and transfer to serving plates. (If you want to make them ahead, they can be kept in an airtight container for up to 2 days.)

5. When you're ready to serve, decorate with a generous squirt of cream then top with kiwi slices and a dusting of sifted icing sugar.

liquid (aquafaba) from a 400g/14oz can of chickpeas/garbanzos

200g/7oz/1 cup caster/superfine sugar

FOR THE TOPPING

ready-whipped vegan cream from a canister

4 kiwi fruits, peeled, sliced and quartered

icing/confectioner's sugar, for dusting

CHOCOLATE MOUSSE

This is such an easy dessert to make – just four ingredients and no cooking. It's incredibly rich and creamy. The avocado does not affect the flavour, it just adds to the delicious creaminess (as well as being really good for you).

SERVES 4–6 * PREP 15 MINS + CHILLING * COOK 5 MINS

1. Position a heatproof bowl over a pan of just-simmering water, making sure the bottom of the bowl doesn't touch the water. Add the chocolate to the bowl and stir occasionally until melted. Leave it to cool a little.
2. Put the avocado, cream, maple syrup and melted chocolate in a food processor and whiz until smooth and combined.
3. Pour the mousse into ramekin dishes and put in the fridge for a couple of hours or overnight to chill and firm up.
4. To serve, top the mousses with grated chocolate and a squirt of cream, if using.

VARIATION

You could add the juice of 1 orange to the chocolate mixture, or a few drops of mint essence if you like mint chocolate!

100g/3¾oz vegan dark/bittersweet chocolate (70% cocoa solids), broken into pieces

1 ripe avocado, halved, stoned and peeled

250ml/8fl oz/1cup vegan single/light cream

1 tbsp maple syrup

FOR THE TOPPING (OPTIONAL)

a grating of vegan dark/bittersweet chocolate (70% cocoa solids)

ready-whipped vegan cream from a canister

BANANA ICE CREAM

This is the simplest instant ice cream made with frozen bananas and a splash of cream, with no churning of any sort required. Even better, it's good for you! Here, it's scooped into cones with a grating of chocolate on top, but you could serve it in a bowl and drizzle over the warm chocolate sauce described below, perhaps with some sliced banana for a very banana-y split.

SERVES 4 * PREP 15 MINS + FREEZING

1. Put the sliced banana in a freezerproof container or bag and put it in the freezer for an hour or so or until they are frozen solid.

2. Put the frozen banana slices in a food processor and pour in the cream or spoon in the yogurt. Whiz in bursts until creamy, but still stiff.

3. Scoop into the cones and grate over some chocolate. Or serve in bowls, perhaps with a warm chocolate sauce.

Warm Chocolate Sauce

150ml/¼ pint/⅔ cup vegan single/light cream

4 tbsp maple syrup

50g/2oz/¼ cup light brown muscovado sugar

40g/1½oz/⅓ cup unsweetened cocoa powder

1 tbsp tahini

75g/3oz/½ cup vegan dark/bittersweet chocolate (70% cocoa solids) chips

1 tsp vanilla extract

1 Pour slightly more than half of the cream into a heavy pan. Add the maple syrup, sugar and cocoa powder. Gently heat, stirring, until the sugar has dissolved and the mixture is smooth, then heat until it begins to boil. Stir continuously as the mixture will start to thicken.

2 Remove from the heat and leave until the bubbles subside, then add the tahini, chocolate chips and vanilla. Stir until the chocolate has melted and the sauce is smooth. Stir in the rest of the cream. Serve warm.

4 bananas, peeled and sliced

4–5 tbsp vegan single/light cream or vegan Greek-style plain yogurt

vegan waffle cones, to serve (optional)

vegan dark/bittersweet chocolate (70% cocoa solids), or warm chocolate sauce (see box), to serve

CHOCOLATE & NUT ICE CREAM

This is a not-too-sweet churned ice cream in which avocados add a wonderful smoothness, although their flavour is barely detectable. If time allows, chill the coconut cream and coconut milk overnight in the fridge. Use coconut evaporated milk in place of coconut milk for a richer result. Leave out the almonds if you prefer.

SERVES 4–6 * PREP 15 MINS + FREEZING

- 150ml/¼ pint/⅔ cup coconut cream
- 400ml/14fl oz can of coconut milk
- 2 small ripe avocados, stoned, peeled and roughly chopped
- about 6 tbsp maple syrup
- 40g/1½oz/⅓ cup unsweetened cocoa powder, sifted
- 1 tsp vanilla extract
- 115g/4oz/1 cup chopped blanched almonds

1. Pour and scrape the coconut cream and coconut milk into a blender or food processor. Add the avocados and maple syrup and blend briefly until the avocados are very finely chopped.
2. Sift in the cocoa powder, add the vanilla, then blend again until the mixture is completely smooth. Taste and add more maple syrup if liked (bear in mind that it will taste slightly less sweet when it's frozen). Stir in the chopped almonds.
3. Churn the mixture in an ice-cream maker until it is firm enough to scoop. Alternatively, pour the mixture into a suitable freezerproof container and freeze it for 1 hour, or until the sides and base are just frozen and the middle is soft. Whisk with a fork for 30 seconds, to break up and combine the frozen and less-frozen parts, then return to the freezer and repeat an hour later. Freeze for at least 2 hours or until solid enough to scoop and serve.

RASPBERRY CREAMSICLES

When the weather hots up, fill your freezer with dairy-free ice lollies for instant refreshment. These creamsicles taste like a frozen smoothie and each counts as two of your five a day! You'll need ice lolly moulds and sticks to make them.

MAKES 8–10 * PREP 15 MINS + FREEZING

1. Put all the ingredients to a liquidizer and whiz until smooth and combined
2. Pour the mixture into the moulds and insert a stick into each one. Put in the freezer for a couple of hours or until completely set.
3. When you want to eat them, run the moulds briefly under warm water to release the creamsicle.

400ml/14fl oz can of coconut milk

300g/11oz/2 cups raspberries, fresh or frozen

2 tbsp vegan plain yogurt

1 tbsp maple syrup

1 tsp vanilla extract

1 banana, peeled and roughly chopped

WATERMELON, LIME & COCONUT
ORANGE & MANGO
BLUEBERRY CREAM

ICE POPS 3 WAYS

Keep a stash of ice pops in your freezer ready to enjoy when the weather turns warm. These popsicles can be served in their silicone moulds, so you can push them up as you eat them. You can also use standard ice lolly moulds with sticks.

ORANGE & MANGO ICE POPS

Tropical mango and orange is a favourite flavour combination, and for good reason. These are sweet and zingy, and super-refreshing.

MAKES 6–8

PREP 5 MINS + FREEZING

300ml/½ pint/1¼ cups fresh orange juice (not from concentrate)

300ml/½ pint/1¼ cups fresh mango juice

1 Mix the juices together, then pour into lolly or ice pop moulds.
2 Put in the freezer for a couple of hours or until frozen. Run the moulds under warm water to release the ice pops.

WATERMELON, LIME & COCONUT POPS

This melon zinger is a little bit different from other ice pops you may have tasted and makes a delicious change.

MAKES 6–8

PREP 5 MINS + FREEZING

200g/7oz watermelon pieces

juice of ½ lime

225ml/8fl oz/1 cup coconut milk

2 tbsp maple syrup

1 Put all the ingredients in a liquidizer and whiz until smooth and combined, then pour the mixture into the lolly or ice pop moulds.
2 Put in the freezer for a couple of hours or until frozen. Run the moulds under warm water to release the ice pops.

BLUEBERRY CREAM POPS

These lip-smacking pops are essentially frozen blueberry milkshake. You can swap the blueberries for other berries if you like – blackberries would be especially delicious.

MAKES 6–8

PREP 5 MINS + FREEZING

120ml/4fl oz/½ cup vegan milk

2 tbsp maple syrup

1 tsp vanilla extract

150g/5oz/1¼ cups blueberries

1 Put all the ingredients in a liquidizer and whiz until smooth and combined. You will still be able to see the blueberry skins. Pour the mixture into the lolly or ice pop moulds.
2 Put in the freezer for a couple of hours or until frozen. Run the moulds under warm water to release the ice pops.

CHOCOLATE BROWNIE ENERGY BALLS

Power balls are really easy to make, taste delicious and are packed with healthy ingredients. Make up a batch and store them in the fridge, then you can just take out as many as you need, when you need them, put them into a smaller container and use them as a portable healthy snack. These ones taste like chocolate brownies!

MAKES 20 * PREP 10 MINS

100g/3¾oz/⅔ cup roasted hazelnuts

100g/3¾oz/1 cup rolled oats

150g/5oz/8 Medjool dates, stoned/pitted

4 tbsp unsweetened cocoa powder

2 tbsp ground flaxseeds

2 tbsp soya protein powder

3 tbsp light olive oil

3–4 tbsp vegan milk

1. Put the toasted hazelnuts and oats in a food processor and blitz until finely chopped. Add the dates, cocoa powder, flaxseeds, protein powder, oil and milk. Blitz until finely chopped and the mixture is beginning to clump together.

2. Squeeze the mixture into a ball, take it out of the processor and cut it into 20 pieces. Roll each piece in the palm of your hands to make a smooth ball.

3. Pack into a plastic container, interleaving the layers with baking parchment. They will store in the fridge for up to 3 days, or you can put them in the freezer for up to a month, taking out balls as you need them and letting them defrost slightly before eating.

Vegan Hack

Protein powder is an excellent way of boosting your nutrient levels, especially if you buy a type that contains a range of vitamins and minerals as well as protein. Add it to power balls, smoothies, porridge, hot chocolate... If you don't have any though, don't worry about it, these balls will taste just as good without.

VERY BERRY ENERGY BALLS

These fruity balls don't contain any nuts so are suitable for school. Frozen berries are a great standby ingredient and are blended with oats, quinoa, seeds and vegan yogurt to make a protein- and vitamin-packed snack for energy on the go. The mint adds summery freshness.

MAKES 20 * PREP 10 MINS

1. Put the oats, quinoa flakes and sunflower seeds in a food processor and blitz until fine.

2. Add the frozen berries, vegan yogurt, agave syrup and mint leaves, and blend until smooth and the mixture has begun to clump together. Leave it to sit for a few minutes to allow some of the moisture to be absorbed and the mixture to thicken up slightly.

3. Scoop the mixture out of the processor and shape it into a soft ball. Cut into about 20 pieces. Roll each piece in the palm of your hands to make a ball.

4. Roll some of the balls in a little coconut if you like, then pack into a plastic container, interleaving the layers with baking parchment. Store in the fridge for up to 3 days, or put them in the freezer (they will keep for up to a month), taking out balls as you need them and leaving them to defrost slightly before eating.

COOK'S NOTES

* If you don't like 'bits' then just blitz for a little longer in the food processor so that the mixture becomes smooth.

* As these contain yogurt, pack into a plastic box with a mini frozen ice block to keep cold or add to an insulated lunch bag to keep them chilled when out and about.

175g/5oz/1¾ cups rolled oats

50g/2oz/⅔ cup quinoa flakes

3 tbsp sunflower seeds

150g/5oz/1 cup frozen mixed berries, no need to defrost

3 tbsp vegan plain yogurt

2 tbsp agave syrup

about 10 fresh mint leaves

a little unsweetened desiccated/dry shredded coconut for rolling (optional)

CHOCOLATE BUTTONS

Forget about sugary-sweet chocolate buttons, these giant-sized chocolate buttons are super-dark and moreish, and fab for grown-ups as well as kids. Top with two different combos of protein-rich nuts and energy-boosting dried fruits.

MAKES 40 * PREP 15 MINS + 10 MINS CHILLING * COOK 4 MINS

1. Line 2 baking sheets with baking parchment. Place a heatproof bowl over a pan of just-simmering water, making sure the bottom of the bowl doesn't touch the water. Add the chocolate to the bowl and stir occasionally until melted.
2. Drop teaspoonfuls of melted chocolate spaced well apart on to the lined sheets and spread with the back of a teaspoon to make circles about 4cm/1½in in diameter.
3. For the nutty-topped buttons, heat a dry frying pan, add the nuts and cook for a minute or two until lightly toasted. Drizzle the maple syrup over and cook for 1–2 minutes more until caramelized. Leave to cool, then spoon the nuts over half of the chocolate buttons and sprinkle with the orange zest before the chocolate sets.
4. For the super-fruity topping, sprinkle the dried fruits over the remaining chocolate buttons before the chocolate sets.
5. Chill both sheets in the fridge for 10 minutes until set. Store any leftovers to a plastic container layered with baking parchment. These will keep in the fridge for up to 3 days.

100g/3¾oz vegan dark/bittersweet chocolate (70% cocoa solids), broken into pieces

FOR A NUTTY TOPPING

2 tbsp pistachio nuts, roughly chopped

2 tbsp unblanched almonds, roughly chopped

4 Brazil nuts, roughly chopped

1 tbsp maple syrup

zest of 1 medium orange, finely grated

FOR A SUPER-FRUITY TOPPING

6 ready-to-eat dried apricots, roughly chopped

1 tbsp dried cranberries, roughly chopped

NUTRITIONAL NOTES

The nutritional analysis is calculated per portion (i.e. serving or item). If the recipe gives a range, such as Serves 4–6, then the nutritional analysis will be for the smaller portion. The analysis does not include optional ingredients, such as salt to taste.

30 **SPAGHETTI VEGANESE** Energy 496kcal/2106kJ; Protein 21g; Carb 96.2g, of which sugars 12.6g; Fat 5.8g, of which saturates 0.7g; Chol 0mg; Calc 85mg; Fibre 11.4g; Sodium 197mg.

33 **PASTA, TOMATO & 'BACON'** Energy 439kcal/1864kJ; Protein 14g; Carb 84.6g, of which sugars 12.3g; Fat 6.3g, of which saturates 0.6g; Chol 0mg; Calc 61mg; Fibre 7.1g; Sodium 60mg.

34 **SPAGHETTI 'CARBONARA'** Energy 713kcal/3000kJ; Protein 50.1g; Carb 94.6g, of which sugars 7.3g; Fat 19.9g, of which saturates 1.1g; Chol 0mg; Calc 266mg; Fibre 10.5g; Sodium 148mg.

37 **COURGETTI WITH PESTO** Energy 379kcal/1567kJ; Protein 6.8g; Carb 15.9g, of which sugars 6g; Fat 32.4g, of which saturates 5.2g; Chol 17mg; Calc 85mg; Fibre 4.1g; Sodium 13mg.

40 **PASTA WITH GREEN PESTO** Energy 671kcal/2816kJ; Protein 24.4g; Carb 84.2g, of which sugars 5.7g; Fat 28.8g, of which saturates 4.9g; Chol 0mg; Calc 95mg; Fibre 9.6g; Sodium 14mg.

43 **PASTA WITH ORANGE PESTO** Energy 839kcal/3519kJ; Protein 22.7g; Carb 93.5g, of which sugars 11.5g; Fat 44.6g, of which saturates 6.5g; Chol 0mg; Calc 101mg; Fibre 10.2g; Sodium 10mg.

44 **PASTA WITH RED PESTO** Energy 753kcal/3155kJ; Protein 20.9g; Carb 86.1g, of which sugars 9.4g; Fat 38.8g, of which saturates 7g; Chol 0mg; Calc 59mg; Fibre 9.3g; Sodium 9mg.

46 **MACARONI CHEESE** Energy 739kcal/3105kJ; Protein 14g; Carb 116.1g, of which sugars 3.4g; Fat 26.8g, of which saturates 10.7g; Chol 3mg; Calc 62mg; Fibre 4.5g; Sodium 190mg.

49 **VEGETABLE LASAGNE** Energy 409kcal/1713kJ; Protein 9.9g; Carb 57.4g, of which sugars 10.9g; Fat 16.6g, of which saturates 2.9g; Chol 18mg; Calc 80mg; Fibre 6.5g; Sodium 126mg.

50 **STICKY TOFU NOODLES** Energy 722kcal/3031kJ; Protein 56.1g; Carb 76.7g, of which sugars 7.9g; Fat 26.1g, of which saturates 1g; Chol 0mg; Calc 421mg; Fibre 9.3g; Sodium 23mg.

53 **VEG NOODLE LASKA** Energy 307kcal/1292kJ; Protein 7.8g; Carb 65g, of which sugars 18.5g; Fat 2.2g, of which saturates 0.5g; Chol 0mg; Calc 205mg; Fibre 8.9g; Sodium 265mg.

54 **EASY MARGARITA PIZZA** Energy 616kcal/2601kJ; Protein 13.2g; Carb 108.6g, of which sugars 6.4g; Fat 17.3g, of which saturates 8.1g; Chol 0mg; Calc 191mg; Fibre 6.9g; Sodium 539mg.

57 **HAWAIIAN PIZZA** Energy 705kcal/2976kJ; Protein 12.9g; Carb 115.9g, of which sugars 9.9g; Fat 22.6g, of which saturates 11.8g; Chol 0mg; Calc 196mg; Fibre 6.9g; Sodium 44mg.

57 **MUSHROOM PEPPER PIZZA** Energy 740kcal/3119kJ; Protein 15.4g; Carb 124.4g, of which sugars 15.4g; Fat 23.5g, of which saturates 14.1g; Chol 0mg; Calc 204mg; Fibre 10.6g; Sodium 52mg.

59 **CALZONE** Energy 612kcal/2582kJ; Protein 13g; Carb 107.3g, of which sugars 5.3g; Fat 17.4g, of which saturates 8.1g; Chol 0mg; Calc 210mg; Fibre 6.9g; Sodium 535mg.

60 **FUN FRIED RICE** Energy 501kcal/2106kJ; Protein 25.7g; Carb 68.5g, of which sugars 16.9g; Fat 15.7g, of which saturates 3.6g; Chol 0mg; Calc 174mg; Fibre 15.7g; Sodium 1110mg.

63 **SUSHI** Energy 241kcal/1006kJ; Protein 8.5g; Carb 39.5g, of which sugars 5.6g; Fat 5.4g, of which saturates 1.1g; Chol 0mg; Calc 106mg; Fibre 11.1g; Sodium 117mg.

64 **SUMMERY RISOTTO** Energy 385kcal/1604kJ; Protein 6.5g; Carb 58.9g, of which sugars 2.9g; Fat 13.6g, of which saturates 6.3g; Chol 21mg; Calc 25mg; Fibre 1.7g; Sodium 68mg.

70 **BEETROOT BURGER** Energy 211kcal/887kJ; Protein 7.3g; Carb 29g, of which sugars 15.4g; Fat 8.1g, of which saturates 0.9g; Chol 3mg; Calc 71mg; Fibre 7.1g; Sodium 178mg.

73 **TOFU BURGER** Energy 190kcal/802kJ; Protein 6.7g; Carb 28.5g, of which sugars 5.6g; Fat 6.3g, of which saturates 0.7g; Chol 0mg; Calc 182mg; Fibre 5.3g; Sodium 184mg.

74 **SOYA BURGER** Energy 233kcal/984kJ; Protein 18.5g; Carb 26.7g, of which sugars 4.5g; Fat 6.5g, of which saturates 0.8g; Chol 0mg; Calc 131mg; Fibre 3.5g; Sodium 1474mg.

77 **FISHLESS FINGERS** Energy 365kcal/1528kJ; Protein 19.6g; Carb 39.4g, of which sugars 2.7g; Fat 15.4g, of which saturates 3.1g; Chol 0mg; Calc 585mg; Fibre 12.6g; Sodium 407mg.

79 **FAT CHIPS** Energy 200kcal/847kJ; Protein 4.3g; Carb 40.3g, of which sugars 3.3g; Fat 3.5g, of which saturates 0.6g; Chol 83mg; Calc 15mg; Fibre 3.3g; Sodium 273mg.

79 **SKINNY FRIES** Energy 200kcal/847kJ; Protein 4.3g; Carb 40.3g, of which sugars 3.3g; Fat 3.5g, of which saturates 0.6g; Chol 83mg; Calc 15mg; Fibre 3.3g; Sodium 28mg.

79 **SWEET POTATO FRIES** Energy 242kcal/1032kJ; Protein 3g; Carb 53.3g, of which sugars 14.3g; Fat 3.5g, of which saturates 0.6g; Chol 0mg; Calc 60mg; Fibre 8g; Sodium 100mg.

80 **CLASSIC BREAKFAST** Energy 569kcal/2387kJ; Protein 20.3g; Carb 54.9g, of which sugars 12.8g; Fat 29.7g, of which saturates 5.9g; Chol 0mg; Calc 224mg; Fibre 7.8g; Sodium 1495mg.

82 **BANGERS & MASH** Energy 217kcal/916kJ; Protein 9.9g; Carb 36.7g, of which sugars 8.9g; Fat 4.4g, of which saturates 0.5g; Chol 0mg; Calc 70mg; Fibre 7.9g; Sodium 578mg.

85 **POTATO MASH** Energy 265kcal/1114kJ; Protein 4.3g; Carb 41.6g, of which sugars 3.4g; Fat 9.9g, of which saturates 3.3g; Chol 113mg; Calc 16mg; Fibre 3.3g; Sodium 127mg.

85 **BEETROOT MASH** Energy 292kcal/1229kJ; Protein 5.6g; Carb 47.3g, of which sugars 8.6g; Fat 10g, of which saturates 3.3g; Chol 113mg; Calc 31mg; Fibre 5.2g; Sodium 176mg.

85 **PESTO & PEA MASH** Energy 345kcal/1446kJ; Protein 8.4g; Carb 45.1g, of which sugars 4g; Fat 15.6g, of which saturates 3.5g; Chol 118mg; Calc 76mg; Fibre 5.1g; Sodium 164mg.

85 **SWEET POTATO MASH** Energy 301kcal/1272kJ; Protein 3g; Carb 53.4g, of which sugars 14.4g; Fat 9.8g, of which saturates 3.3g; Chol 31mg; Calc 61mg; Fibre 8g; Sodium 199mg.

86 **CORN WITH CHILLI BUTTER** Energy 313kcal/1301kJ; Protein 3.9g; Carb 18.6g, of which sugars 3g; Fat 24.9g, of which saturates 8g; Chol 79mg; Calc 7mg; Fibre 2.2g; Sodium 256mg.

86 **CORN WITH HERBY BUTTER** Energy 314kcal/1305kJ; Protein 4g; Carb 18.5g, of which sugars 2.7g; Fat 25g, of which saturates 8g; Chol 79mg; Calc 30mg; Fibre 3g; Sodium 259mg.

86 **CORN WITH TEX-MEX BUTTER** Energy 313kcal/1298kJ; Protein 3.8g; Carb 18.5g, of which sugars 2.5g; Fat 24.9g, of which saturates 8g; Chol 79mg; Calc 6mg; Fibre 2.2g; Sodium 255mg.

89 **TOFU KEBABS** Energy 159kcal/663kJ; Protein 10.1g; Carb 19.4g, of which sugars 17.9g; Fat 4.9g, of which saturates 0.7g; Chol 0mg; Calc 505mg; Fibre 4.6g; Sodium 554mg.

90 **VEG TEMPURA** Energy 280kcal/1170kJ; Protein 7.4g; Carb 35.3g, of which sugars 12.5g; Fat 12.9g, of which saturates 1.7g; Chol 0mg; Calc 89mg; Fibre 7.9g; Sodium 26mg.

93 **SWEETCORN FRITTERS** Energy 154kcal/651kJ; Protein 4.9g; Carb 22.4g, of which sugars 2.6g; Fat 5.7g, of which saturates 0.7g; Chol 0mg; Calc 23mg; Fibre 4g; Sodium 14mg.

94 **COURGETTE FRITTERS** Energy 234kcal/974kJ; Protein 3.7g; Carb 21.7g, of which sugars 2.5g; Fat 15.2g, of which saturates 8.7g; Chol 0mg; Calc 45mg; Fibre 2.6g; Sodium 9mg.

97 **COCONUT PATTIES** Energy 110kcal/455kJ; Protein 2.1g; Carb 5.6g, of which sugars 1.6g; Fat 8.9g, of which saturates 7.4g; Chol 0mg; Calc 14mg; Fibre 2g; Sodium 23mg.

98 **TOFU HOISIN HOT PITTA** Energy 325kcal/1372kJ; Protein 15.6g; Carb 50.5g, of which sugars 10.1g; Fat 8.1g, of which saturates 1g; Chol 0mg; Calc 598mg; Fibre 3.7g; Sodium 392mg.

101 **PULLED JACKFRUIT WRAPS** Energy 459kcal/1924kJ; Protein 6.6g; Carb 63.8g, of which sugars 30.9g; Fat 21.5g, of which saturates 4.3g; Chol 0mg; Calc 86mg; Fibre 6.7g; Sodium 421mg.

102 **CHINESE PANCAKES** Energy 102kcal/433kJ; Protein 2.1g; Carb 17.2g, of which sugars 2.6g; Fat 2.4g, of which saturates 0.2g; Chol 0mg; Calc 34mg; Fibre 1.2g; Sodium 153mg.

105 **QUESADILLAS** Energy 465kcal/1957kJ; Protein 8.1g; Carb 74.5g, of which sugars 3.9g; Fat 17g, of which saturates 12.4g; Chol 0mg; Calc 126mg; Fibre 4.3g; Sodium 297mg.

106 **TOASTIES** Energy 266kcal/1118kJ; Protein 12.3g; Carb 30.5g, of which sugars 2.5g; Fat 11.4g, of which saturates 4.3g; Chol 0mg; Calc 160mg; Fibre 2g; Sodium 681mg.

109 **THE VLT** Energy 386kcal/1610kJ; Protein 5.2g; Carb 25.5g, of which sugars 4g; Fat 25.7g, of which saturates 3g; Chol 21mg; Calc 95mg; Fibre 2.4g; Sodium 299mg.

110 **ALMOST EGG & CRESS** Energy 278kcal/1165kJ; Protein 9.1g; Carb 33.7g, of which sugars 1.5g; Fat 12.8g, of which saturates 1.9g; Chol 16mg; Calc 113mg; Fibre 4.7g; Sodium 423mg.

111 **BEAN & PESTO PASTE** Energy 248kcal/1046kJ; Protein 11.2g; Carb 37.5g, of which sugars 5.8g; Fat 7g, of which saturates 0.4g; Chol 5mg; Calc 199mg; Fibre 7.9g; Sodium 547mg.

114 **CHESTNUT ROAST** Energy 196kcal/826kJ; Protein 4.8g; Carb 36.9g, of which sugars 4g; Fat 4.2g, of which saturates 0.4g; Chol 0mg; Calc 61mg; Fibre 2.3g; Sodium 240mg.

117 **ALL THE TRIMMINGS** Energy 1132kcal/4729kJ; Protein 38.6g; Carb 108g, of which sugars 25.5g; Fat 62.8g, of which saturates 20.1g; Chol 143mg; Calc 380mg; Fibre 23g; Sodium 2446mg.

119 **VEGAN TOAD IN THE HOLE** Energy 394kcal/1655kJ; Protein 18.4g; Carb 45.4g, of which sugars 1.8g; Fat 16.5g, of which saturates 3.1g; Chol 0mg; Calc 267mg; Fibre 1.6g; Sodium 1030mg.

120 **CAJUN TRAY BAKE** Energy 359kcal/1510kJ; Protein 27.6g; Carb 40g, of which sugars 10.8g; Fat 11.1g, of which saturates 1.5g; Chol 33mg; Calc 154mg; Fibre 4.5g; Sodium 2353mg.

123 **CHEESY NACHOS BAKE** Energy 407kcal/1701kJ; Protein 8.3g; Carb 35.9g, of which sugars 4.7g; Fat 26.4g, of which saturates 8.1g; Chol 0mg; Calc 96mg; Fibre 9.4g; Sodium 466mg.

124 **ROAST VEGETABLE TIKKA** Energy 223kcal/941kJ; Protein 13.1g; Carb 28.2g, of which sugars 13.4g; Fat 7.2g, of which saturates 1g; Chol 0mg; Calc 194mg; Fibre 13.2g; Sodium 139mg.

127 **SAMOSAS** Energy 130kcal/546.6kJ; Protein 3.06g; Carb 18g, of which sugars 1.62g; Fat 5.58g, of which saturates 0.66g; Chol 0.4mg; Calc 39mg; Fibre 2g; Sodium 234mg.

128 **SAUSAGE-LESS ROLLS** Energy 345kcal/1434kJ; Protein 5.4g; Carb 21.2g, of which sugars 3.1g; Fat 27.1g, of which saturates 6.2g; Chol 20mg; Calc 53mg; Fibre 1.7g; Sodium 752mg.

131 **CHILLI 'NON' CARNE** Energy 457kcal/1926kJ; Protein 53.5g; Carb 37.8g, of which sugars 15.4g; Fat 11.2g, of which saturates 1.5g; Chol 0mg; Calc 291mg; Fibre 5g; Sodium 4990mg.

132 **COTTAGE PIE** Energy 457kcal/1922kJ; Protein 14.2g; Carb 70.4g, of which sugars 15.9g; Fat 15g, of which saturates 2.9g; Chol 75mg; Calc 137mg; Fibre 16.9g; Sodium 651mg.

135 **VEGETABLE MOUSSAKA** Energy 223kcal/928kJ; Protein 11.2g; Carb 14.9g, of which sugars 12.3g; Fat 13.6g, of which saturates 1.5g; Chol 0mg; Calc 311mg; Fibre 6.2g; Sodium 221mg.

136 **JACKFRUIT HOTPOT** Energy 464kcal/1944kJ; Protein 6.2g; Carb 60.9g, of which sugars 17.9g; Fat 23.4g, of which saturates 10.1g; Chol 4mg; Calc 201mg; Fibre 6.2g; Sodium 524mg.

139 **SPICY TOFU STIR-UP** Energy 208kcal/863kJ; Protein 7.8; Carb 14g, of which sugars 5.8g; Fat 15, of which saturates 1.6g; Chol 14mg; Calc 316mg; Fibre 3.9g; Sodium 30mg.

140 **KORMA CURRY** Energy 458kcal/1924kJ; Protein 18g; Carb 52.7g, of which sugars 21.3g; Fat 21.6g, of which saturates 1.5g; Chol 0mg; Calc 240mg; Fibre 17.3g; Sodium 255mg.

143 **MUSHROOM STROGANOFF** Energy 356kcal/1486kJ; Protein 12.9g; Carb 6.6g, of which sugars 4g; Fat 29g, of which saturates 3.6g; Chol 0mg; Calc 30mg; Fibre 3g; Sodium 83mg.

144 **TOMATO NO-MEAT BAKE** Energy 396kcal/1658kJ; Protein 12.3g; Carb 46.8g, of which sugars 15.3g; Fat 19.1g, of which saturates 2.1g; Chol 0mg; Calc 120mg; Fibre 11.4g; Sodium 874mg.

147 **SWEDISH MEATLESS BALLS** Energy 523kcal/2193kJ; Protein 13.2g; Carb 71.1g, of which sugars 10.9g; Fat 22.5g, of which saturates 2.6g; Chol 62mg; Calc 96mg; Fibre 11.1g; Sodium 1237mg.

148 **TOMATO SOUP** Energy 246kcal/1030kJ; Protein 4g; Carb 29.8g, of which sugars 9.2g; Fat 13.2g, of which saturates 7g; Chol 0mg; Calc 65mg; Fibre 4g; Sodium 169mg.

151 **SWEETCORN SOUP** Energy 394kcal/1655kJ; Protein 6.7g; Carb 82g, of which sugars 10g; Fat 4.1g, of which saturates 0.5g; Chol 0mg; Calc 23mg; Fibre 2.3g; Sodium 530mg.

155 **ORANGE SMOOTHIE** Energy 159kcal/675kJ; Protein 4.2g; Carb 36.4g, of which sugars 35.7g; Fat 0.7g, of which saturates 0.2g; Chol 0mg; Calc 176mg; Fibre 11.2g; Sodium 50mg.

155 **BERRY NICE SMOOTHIE** Energy 221kcal/927kJ; Protein 3.1g; Carb 45.7g, of which sugars 28g; Fat 3.6g, of which saturates 0.2g; Chol 0mg; Calc 35mg; Fibre 3g; Sodium 22mg.

155 **GORGEOUS GREEN** Energy 55kcal/234kJ; Protein 1.3g; Carb 12.5g, of which sugars 11.7g; Fat 0.4g, of which saturates 0.1g; Chol 0mg; Calc 46mg; Fibre 2g; Sodium 37mg.

158 **SAVOURY BAGELS** Energy 436kcal/1836kJ; Protein 25.9g; Carb 56.7g, of which sugars 6.7g; Fat 13.4g, of which saturates 1.1g; Chol 0mg; Calc 492mg; Fibre 3.3g; Sodium 768mg.

161 **FRENCH TOAST** Energy 378kcal/1578kJ; Protein 4.8g; Carb 41.6g, of which sugars 9.6g; Fat 22g, of which saturates 7g; Chol 69mg; Calc 62mg; Fibre 1.1g; Sodium 507mg.

162 **PANCAKES** Energy 172kcal/727kJ; Protein 3.5g; Carb 35.6g, of which sugars 2.5g; Fat 2.6g, of which saturates 0.2g; Chol 0mg; Calc 132mg; Fibre 1.6g; Sodium 135mg.

165 **GARLIC BREAD** Energy 306kcal/1271kJ; Protein 3.6g; Carb 19.6g, of which sugars 1.4g; Fat 23.8g, of which saturates 8g; Chol 79mg; Calc 43mg; Fibre 1g; Sodium 448mg.

165 **RED PESTO BREAD** Energy 163kcal/687kJ; Protein 6g; Carb 18.9g, of which sugars 1g; Fat 7.7g, of which saturates 0.2g; Chol 6mg; Calc 114mg; Fibre 0.8g; Sodium 245mg.

166 **MINI POTATO SKINS** Energy 212kcal/889kJ; Protein 2.9g; Carb 27.9g, of which sugars 5.6g; Fat 10.6g, of which saturates 4.9g; Chol 28mg; Calc 14mg; Fibre 2.3g; Sodium 116mg.

169 **CAULI MUNCHIES** Energy 156kcal/652kJ; Protein 7.6g; Carb 13.3g, of which sugars 9.8g; Fat 8.5g, of which saturates 1.3g; Chol 0mg; Calc 71mg; Fibre 4g; Sodium 29mg.

170 **MOZZARELLA STICKS** Energy 84kcal/349kJ; Protein 1.1g; Carb 9.5g, of which sugars 0.2g; Fat 4.8g, of which saturates 2.8g; Chol 0mg; Calc 10mg; Fibre 0.2g; Sodium 35mg.

173 **HUMMUS** Energy 300kcal/1240kJ; Protein 4.5g; Carb 7g, of which sugars 0.2g; Fat 28.3g, of which saturates 3.9g; Chol 0mg; Calc 19mg; Fibre 2.4g; Sodium 95mg.

173 **RED PEPPER HUMMUS** Energy 505kcal/2095kJ; Protein 8.6g; Carb 21.7g, of which sugars 10.9g; Fat 43.2g, of which saturates 6.1g; Chol 0mg; Calc 42mg; Fibre 7.3g; Sodium 150mg.

173 **GUACAMOLE** Energy 212kcal/877kJ; Protein 2.4g; Carb 3.1g, of which sugars 1.2g; Fat 21.3g, of which saturates 4.5g; Chol 0mg; Calc 14mg; Fibre 5.3g; Sodium 8mg.

177 **CHILLI CASHEWS** Energy 221kcal/915kJ; Protein 6.9g; Carb 7.5g, of which sugars 1.7g; Fat 18.3g, of which saturates 3.6g; Chol 0mg; Calc 16mg; Fibre 1.6g; Sodium 6mg.

177 **SALTED ALMONDS** Energy 233kcal/963kJ; Protein 7.9g; Carb 2.6g, of which sugars 1.6g; Fat 21.3g, of which saturates 1.7g; Chol 0mg; Calc 90mg; Fibre 0g; Sodium 333mg.

177 **MAPLE PECANS** Energy 285kcal/1176kJ; Protein 3.5g; Carb 8.9g, of which sugars 7.7g; Fat 26.3g, of which saturates 2.1g; Chol 0mg; Calc 30mg; Fibre 2.4g; Sodium 1mg.

178 **QUICK-ROAST CHICKPEAS** Energy 106kcal/445kJ; Protein 6g; Carb 13.5g, of which sugars 1.8g; Fat 4.6g, of which saturates 0.5g; Chol 0mg; Calc 97mg; Fibre 3.6g; Sodium 149mg.

181 **VEG CRISPS** Energy 222kcal/929kJ; Protein 4g; Carb 24.5g, of which sugars 13.8g; Fat 12.7g, of which saturates 1.9g; Chol 0mg; Calc 77mg; Fibre 11.1g; Sodium 556mg.

183 **SALTED POPCORN** Energy 82kcal/339kJ; Protein 0.9g; Carb 6.7g, of which sugars 0.2g; Fat 5.9g, of which saturates 0.6g; Chol 0mg; Calc 2mg; Fibre 0g; Sodium 492mg.

183 **SWEET POPCORN** Energy 538kcal/2219kJ; Protein 1g; Carb 16.8g, of which sugars 9.3g; Fat 52.2g, of which saturates 23.1g; Chol 8mg; Calc 14mg; Fibre 0g; Sodium 334mg.

183 **SALTY & SWEET** Energy 310kcal/1279kJ; Protein 0.9g; Carb 11.7g, of which sugars 4.7g; Fat 29.1g, of which saturates 11.9g; Chol 4mg; Calc 8mg; Fibre 0g; Sodium 413mg.

186 **CHOCOLATE CAKE** Energy 540kcal/2257kJ; Protein 3.3g; Carb 61.6g, of which sugars 42.7g; Fat 32.8g, of which saturates 13g; Chol 4mg; Calc 87mg; Fibre 1.8g; Sodium 609mg.

191 **VANILLA SPONGE CAKE** Energy 453kcal/1899kJ; Protein 3.8g; Carb 61.8g, of which sugars 35.1g; Fat 22.7g, of which saturates 8.4g; Chol 3mg; Calc 127mg; Fibre 1.5g; Sodium 238mg.

193 **BASIC CUPCAKE MIXTURE** Energy 174kcal/741kJ; Protein 2.4g; Carb 42g, of which sugars 21g; Fat 0.7g, of which saturates 0.1g; Chol 0mg; Calc 94mg; Fibre 1.1g; Sodium 92mg.

193 **SIMPLE VANILLA CAKES** Energy 272kcal/1160kJ; Protein 2.4g; Carb 68.2g, of which sugars 47g; Fat 0.7g, of which saturates 0.1g; Chol 0mg; Calc 94mg; Fibre 1.1g; Sodium 95mg.

196 **LEMON BUTTERFLY CAKES** Energy 416kcal/1752kJ; Protein 2.5g; Carb 68.4g, of which sugars 47.2g; Fat 16.2g, of which saturates 5.3g; Chol 53mg; Calc 95mg; Fibre 1.1g; Sodium 266mg.

196 **CHOCOLATE MAPLE CAKES** Energy 424kcal/1783kJ; Protein 2.6g; Carb 69.1g, of which sugars 47.7g; Fat 17g, of which saturates 3.5g; Chol 0mg; Calc 97mg; Fibre 1.2g; Sodium 238mg.

199 **LEMON DRIZZLE CAKE** Energy 341kcal/1444kJ; Protein 3.8g; Carb 65.1g, of which sugars 39.4g; Fat 9.1g, of which saturates 1.1g; Chol 0mg; Calc 134mg; Fibre 1.6g; Sodium 474mg.

200 **PUMPKIN TRAYBAKE** Energy 247kcal/1040kJ; Protein 3g; Carb 38.8g, of which sugars 20.1g; Fat 9.8g, of which saturates 3g; Chol 29mg; Calc 46mg; Fibre 1.3g; Sodium 148mg.

205 **CHOCOLATE BROWNIES** Energy 293kcal/1224kJ; Protein 2.6g; Carb 33g, of which sugars 25.1g; Fat 17.4g, of which saturates 7.3g; Chol 41mg; Calc 29mg; Fibre 1.6g; Sodium 170mg.

206 **FLAPJACK** Energy 313kcal/1308kJ; Protein 3g; Carb 38.3g, of which sugars 19.8g; Fat 17.4g, of which saturates 7.5g; Chol 3mg; Calc 19mg; Fibre 2.1g; Sodium 119mg.

209 **CHOC SHORTBREADS** Energy 135kcal/563kJ; Protein 1.4g; Carb 15.8g, of which sugars 7.4g; Fat 7.6g, of which saturates 3g; Chol 20mg; Calc 19mg; Fibre 0.7g; Sodium 64mg.

210 **CHOC CHIP COOKIES** Energy 184kcal/774kJ; Protein 1.6g; Carb 25.5g, of which sugars 16.9g; Fat 9.1g, of which saturates 4.7g; Chol 2mg; Calc 22mg; Fibre 0.8g; Sodium 46mg.

213 **PEANUT BUTTER COOKIES** Energy 92kcal/386kJ; Protein 1.1g; Carb 11.6g, of which sugars 6.8g; Fat 4.9g, of which saturates 2.1g; Chol 1mg; Calc 11mg; Fibre 0.3g; Sodium 35mg.

214 **NO-BAKE CHEESECAKE** Energy 631kcal/2627kJ; Protein 6.9g; Carb 40.8g, of which sugars 20g; Fat 49.4g, of which saturates 24.2g; Chol 65mg; Calc 84mg; Fibre 0g; Sodium 451mg.

217 **MINI MERINGUES** Energy 116kcal/494kJ; Protein 0.8g; Carb 27.2g, of which sugars 26.3g; Fat 1.2g, of which saturates 0.2g; Chol 0mg; Calc 11mg; Fibre 0.3g; Sodium 64mg.

218 **CHOCOLATE MOUSSE** Energy 245kcal/1024kJ; Protein 4.9g; Carb 12.7g, of which sugars 12.1g; Fat 19g, of which saturates 5g; Chol 1mg; Calc 10mg; Fibre 1.7g; Sodium 3mg.

221 **BANANA ICE CREAM** Energy 106kcal/449kJ; Protein 1.5g; Carb 25.1g, of which sugars 22.7g; Fat 0.6g, of which saturates 0.2g; Chol 0mg; Calc 8mg; Fibre 1.6g; Sodium 5mg.

222 **CHOC NUT ICE CREAM** Energy 482kcal/2001kJ; Protein 8.5g; Carb 18.3g, of which sugars 11.6g; Fat 43.4g, of which saturates 10.6g; Chol 0mg; Calc 71mg; Fibre 4.6g; Sodium 80mg.

225 **RASPBERRY CREAMSICLES** Energy 113kcal/475kJ; Protein 1.5g; Carb 7.1g, of which sugars 4.4g; Fat 9.7g, of which saturates 0g; Chol 0mg; Calc 9mg; Fibre 2.3g; Sodium 7mg.

227 **ORANGE MANGO ICE POPS** Energy 29kcal/124kJ; Protein 0.3g; Carb 7.2g, of which sugars 7.2g; Fat 0.1g, of which saturates 0g; Chol 0mg; Calc 7mg; Fibre 0.1g; Sodium 7mg.

227 **WATERMELON ICE POPS** Energy 24kcal/101kJ; Protein 0.2g; Carb 5.7g, of which sugars 5.4g; Fat 0.2g, of which saturates 0.1g; Chol 0mg; Calc 12mg; Fibre 0g; Sodium 32mg.

227 **BLUEBERRY CREAM POPS** Energy 29kcal/121kJ; Protein 0g; Carb 6.9g, of which sugars 4.3g; Fat 0.3g, of which saturates 0g; Chol 0mg; Calc 3mg; Fibre 0.6g; Sodium 1mg.

228 **CHOCOLATE ENERGY BALLS** Energy 110kcal/461kJ; Protein 3.1g; Carb 9.5g, of which sugars 4.5g; Fat 7g, of which saturates 0.9g; Chol 0mg; Calc 19mg; Fibre 2.3g; Sodium 31mg.

231 **BERRY ENERGY BALLS** Energy 95kcal/398kJ; Protein 2.8g; Carb 8.9g, of which sugars 2.0g; Fat 1.7g, of which saturates 0.1g; Chol 0mg; Calc 5mg; Fibre 1.7g; Sodium 2mg

232 **CHOCOLATE BUTTONS** Energy 35kcal/131kJ; Protein 0.7g; Carb 2.5g, of which sugars 2.4g; Fat 2.2g, of which saturates 0.7g; Chol 0mg; Calc 7mg; Fibre 0.2g; Sodium 1mg

INDEX

This edition is published by
Lorenz Books, an imprint of
Anness Publishing Ltd

www.annesspublishing.com

info@anness.com

A CIP catalogue record for this book is available from the British Library.

Publisher: Joanna Lorenz

Designer: Simon Daley

Editor: Lucy Doncaster

Photography: William Shaw

Food Stylist: Heather Whinney

Nutritional consultant: Clare Emery

Index: Marie Lorimer

Production Controller: Ben Worley

Please note

If anyone in your family has a health condition, such as diabetes or allergies, it is vital to talk to a doctor or nutritionist before adopting a vegan diet. The advice and recipes are not aimed at babies, toddlers or very young children, who have specific requirements beyond the scope of this book.

COOK'S NOTES

* For all recipes, quantities are given in metric, imperial measures and where appropriate, measures are also given in standard cups and spoons. Follow one set, but not a mixture because they are not interchangeable.
* Standard spoon and cup measures are level. 1 tsp = 5ml, 1 tbsp = 15ml, 1 cup = 250ml/8fl oz. Australian standard tablespoons are 20ml.
* American pints are 16fl oz/2 cups. US readers should use 20fl oz/2.5 cups in place of 1 pint when measuring liquids.
* Australian readers should use 3 tsp in place of 1 tbsp for measuring small quantities.
* Since ovens vary, you should check with your manufacturer's instruction book for guidance.